Walks in the footsteps of Daphne du Maurier

© Sue Kittow, 2018

All Rights Reserved. No part of this publication may be reproduced, stored in a retrieval system, or transmitted in any form or by any means – electronic, mechanical, photocopying, recording, or otherwise – without prior written permission from the publisher or a licence permitting restricted copying issued by the Copyright Licensing Agency, 90 Tottenham Court Road, London W1P 0LA. This book may not be lent, resold, hired out or otherwise disposed of by trade in any form of binding or cover other than that in which it is published, without the prior consent of the publisher.

Moral Rights: The author has asserted her moral right to be identified as the Author of this Work.

Published by Sigma Leisure – an imprint of Sigma Press, Stobart House, Pontyclerc, Penybanc Road, Ammanford, Carmarthenshire SA18 3HP.

British Library Cataloguing in Publication Data
A CIP record for this book is available from the British Library.

ISBN: 978-1-910758-38-0

Typesetting and Design by: Sigma Press, Ammanford.

Cover photographs: View of Poldridmouth and Gribben © Sue Kittow

Photographs: © Sue Kittow, unless otherwise stated

Maps: © Sigma Press
Contains OS data © Crown copyright [and database right] 2018

Printed by: TJ International Ltd, Padstow, Cornwall

Disclaimer: the information in this book is given in good faith and is believed to be correct at the time of publication. No responsibility is accepted by either the author or publisher for errors or omissions, or for any loss or injury however caused. Only you can judge your own fitness, competence and experience. Do not rely solely on sketch maps for navigation: we strongly recommend the use of appropriate Ordnance Survey (or equivalent) maps.

Walks in the footsteps of Daphne du Maurier

Sue Kittow

To the dear friends who accompanied me on these walks, pored over maps and helped keep me going, in alphabetical order: Mel Bailey, Carol Rea and Pilot, Deb Davis, Heather Hosking, Colin Ivens, Rich Milner, Fiona Sanders, Viv Simmons and Titch.

Not forgetting my special shadow, my Moll.

And a special tribute to Paul Burton, who loved walking the Cornish paths, particularly in Penwith.

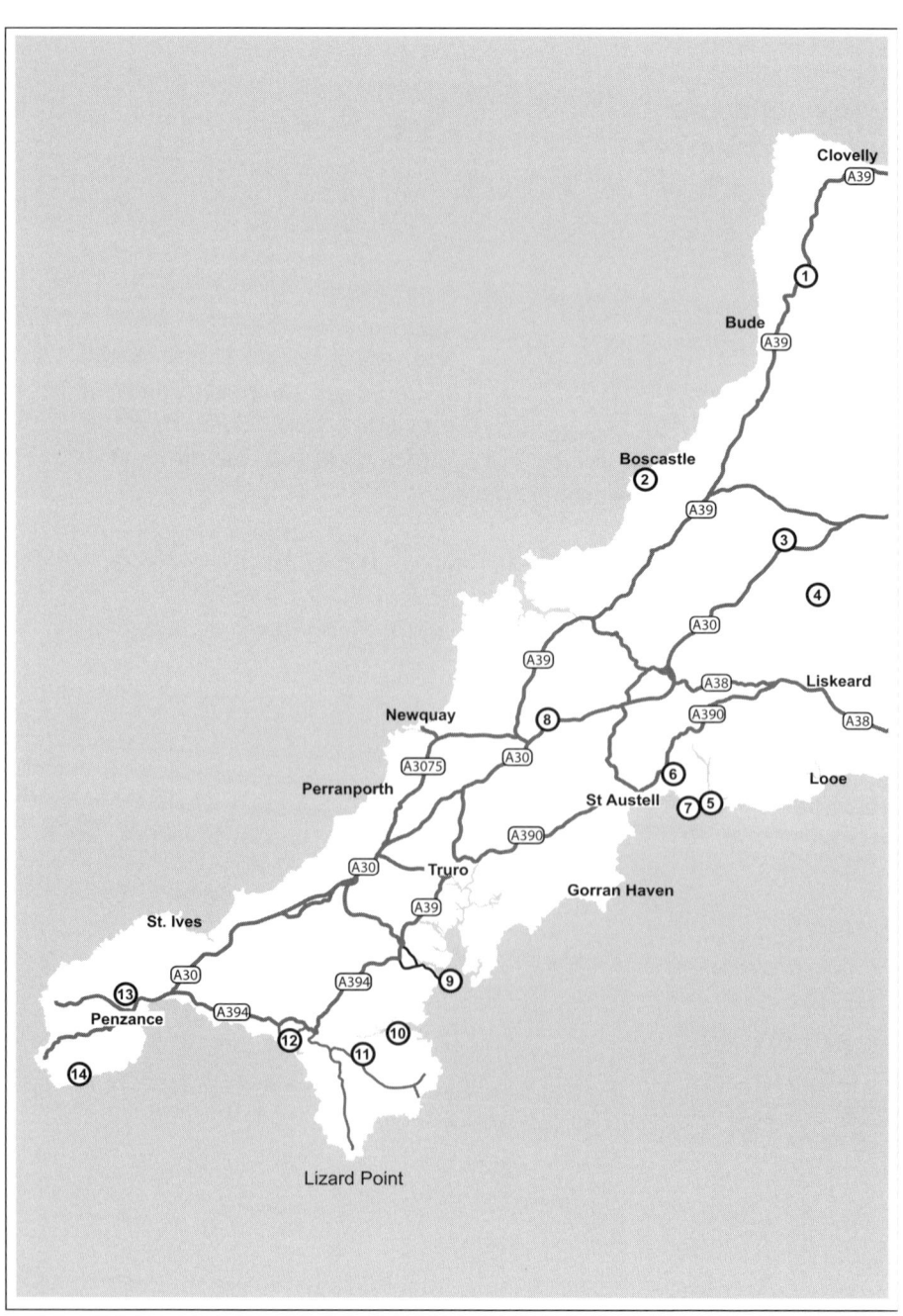

CONTENTS

INTRODUCTION 9
ACKNOWLEDGEMENTS 12
GENERAL INFORMATION 13

THE WALKS

1. STOWE BARTON - KILKHAMPTON, NEAR BUDE 17
   The starting point for The King's General

2. ST NECTAN - ST NECTAN'S GLEN AND KIEVE 28
   Cornish eccentrics and saints from Vanishing Cornwall

3. IN THE SHADOW OF KILMAR TOR 39
   The birthplace of the Merlyn family from Jamaica Inn

4. ALTARNUN 48
   From Jamaica Inn *– The Inny Valleys walk of many stiles*

5. LANTEGLOS CHURCH AND THE HALL WALK 58
   One of Daphne's regular walks, including the church where she married

6. KILMARTH 68
   The inspiration for The House on the Strand

7. GRIBBIN HEAD 77
   Daphne's regular stamping ground from Menabilly

8. CASTLE-AN-DINAS 86
   Location for the dramatic ending of Castle Dor

9. **PENDENNIS CASTLE**   96
From *The King's General*

10. **FRENCHMAN'S CREEK - HELFORD**   106
The setting for the novel

11. **TRELOWARREN - THE HALLIGGYE WALK**   115
The estate that inspired Navron in *Frenchman's Creek*

12. **LOE BAR/POOL**   124
The setting for the end of *Frenchman's Creek*

13. **MADRON WELL - CORNISH SUPERSTITIONS**   135
From *Vanishing Cornwall*

14. **THE LEGEND OF PENROSE**   143
A story of murder and betrayal from *Vanishing Cornwall*

INTRODUCTION

It is well known that Daphne du Maurier fell in love with Fowey as an 18 year old when she visited with her family on the Bodinnick Ferry. "The full expanse of Fowey harbour was beneath us", she wrote. "The whole vista was like a gateway to another world. Here, I thought, was the freedom I had sought, and not yet found. Here was the freedom and solace to walk, sail, go fishing, and even perhaps to write."

Both sides of my family are Cornish, and athough I was born in London and brought up over the Tamar, in Devon, my grandmother still lived in Camborne, so we visited regularly. I, too, fell in love with Fowey in my late twenties, visiting from London, where I worked in television. When the big recession of 1990 hit, I was made redundant, and it proved impossible to get any work in London, so I let out my flat and did a recce in Fowey where I secured a job at the local Spar shop, and found a flat to live in.

The job didn't last long as I am innumerate and couldn't work the till, but I stayed in Fowey for another year, doing odd jobs, and walking a lot, seduced by the magical peace of the town, particularly in winter. I loved the quietness of the dark green river, lapping at the steep, wooded banks. While I had no access to a boat, I explored the coastline as Daphne had. I bought a book on local walks and decided to do one a day, to keep depression at bay.

Lack of work drove me away from Cornwall for a few years, but Fowey has always been a haven to me, and I have often returned, out of season. At the end of a week's holiday there, in March 2010, I was walking along the coastal footpath from Coombe Farm, when I had a sudden premonition that my husband would die. It was almost an out of body experience, but because I was near my beloved Fowey, I felt reassured that whenever it happened, I would be all right. And it wouldn't be for ages, anyway.

Sadly he did die, much sooner than I expected, on Boxing Day that year, but Fowey always has – and I hope always will – be my solace. Just as it was for Daphne du Maurier.

One theme that runs through several of her novels is that of fugitives. By 1942 Daphne was having an affair with Christopher Puxley, a quiet, gentle, good looking man who played the piano beautifully. A very different man to her husband: a complex soldier who loved sailing and walking.

Cornwall was definitely Daphne's refuge, and Menabilly in particular, so for Donna St Columb, the heroine of *Frenchman's Creek*, Navron became her place to escape from the boredom and horrors of London. Like Daphne, Donna longed to be a man and dresses up as a pirate on one escapade. Like Donna, Daphne knew herself to be in love (the French pirate bears a close resemblance to Christopher), but at no time did she ever feel that her marriage was threatened. The pirate also seeks refuge from his home in Finisterre, coming to Cornwall to spend the odd night at Navron, while it was empty, and dream about the owner's wife, while he amused himself outwitting the Cornish gentry.

In *House on the Strand*, Dick retreats to his friend's house in Tywardreath to escape from his marriage, and then enters a previously unknown world of the 14th century.

In *Jamaica Inn*, Mary Yellan is an unwilling fugitive from the quiet lanes of the Helford, finding herself at the terrifying Jamaica Inn. So she escapes to the wildness of Twelve Men's Moor – which leads her to the strange Vicar of Altarnun, and to her uncle's brother, Joss Merlyn. Richard Grenvile, The King's General in the novel of the same name, commands the King's forces but constantly returns to Cornwall to see his beloved Honor and escape from the mayhem of war.

Don't we all seek escapism in some form or other? I certainly do, and find walking, and treading in the paths of Donna St Columb, Mary Yellan or Dick Young, a wonderful way to do so.

While writing the introduction – which I tend to do last, when I've written all the walks, I worry – would Daphne du Maurier be pleased with what I've written? How can I possibly do justice to her work? I can almost hear her stirring in her grave, voice rising in anger at some point that I had not understood, or misinterpreted. So my biggest hope is that this book does justice to a writer that I think is unequalled in her descriptions of the Cornish landscape, of the tides and waters, of the wildlife and moors of this extraordinary county that I am fortunate enough to live in.

Her ability to evoke the landscape always makes me gasp, no matter how often I read her novels (and it has been often, over the many years since I discovered her). She can still terrify me with her description of Joss Merlyn's huge hands cutting a delicate slice of bread for Mary Yellan at the beginning of *Jamaica Inn*. I always cry at the end of *Frenchman's Creek*, picturing them sitting on the shore side at Loe Bar. Honor's courage makes me sit up a little straighter, when I read *The King's General*, and I can never visit Tywardreath without thinking of the Benedictine Priory that existed there, many years ago.

Finishing a book is a mixture of relief and achievement (to have met the deadline), intense grief (at having finished) and disappointment (at having finished, having enjoyed the whole process). "Like giving birth?" asked my mother. Possibly, but unlike giving birth, once a manuscript is winging its way to my publishers, I panic unless I have another project (book) on the go. It's more like being an addict than any maternal instincts.

Every book, however, like children or pets, has its own character. This is formed partly by my research – which novels I have read in the process, how I felt about the characters and stories. Partly by what I have learned about the writer as I research – how I identify with him or her. Each walk has its own character, too, depending on who came with me, what the weather was like, the time of year, and what was happening in each of our lives. The food we took with us, whether we stopped for a drink along the way, or at the end. What we wore, what moods we were in, whether we got lost, wet, blown by wind or rain, tripped and got twisted ankles, or ran out of petrol.

Transcribing each walk is a poignant reminder of all of these things, and is another way to relive the experience, particularly noting things such as a person's voice, the insistence of a bird's call, an interesting bit of gossip, a note to remind me to do something completely different. While you might miss out on the gossip, I only hope you enjoy these walks as much as we have.

This, my fourth book, now takes place alongside the other three. A growing family, and one that I am somewhat amazed by. Did I really write these books? And, more incredibly, do people still want to buy them? Yes I did, and I sincerely hope you, the reader, will continue to want to buy them. Please do get in touch with any comments – I always love to hear from you.

Sue Kittow
April 2018

ACKNOWLEDGEMENTS

To my loyal proof readers, in alphabetical order: David and Jenny Dearlove, Av Harcourt, Colin Ivens and Shelagh Smith.
To John Roberts for those all important grid references.
To Tony Foster for valuable tide and general seagoing information.

GENERAL INFORMATION

- These walks vary in length, so take note according to how much time you have available.

- When out walking, wear appropriate footwear and clothing as weather conditions can change very quickly – rain, fog or even sunshine can descend at a moment's notice.

- Take a mobile phone with you, but be aware that there are many places without a signal, so tell others when and where you are going – and when you return.

- The cliff path is hazardous to dogs who may chase birds and rabbits etc., so keep dogs on a lead near the cliff edge.

- Cornwall is littered with mine shafts, so be careful.

- While the maps contained in this book are as accurate as possible, it is advisable to take the relevant Ordnance Survey map or use one of the OS apps on your phone.

- It's possible you may get lost, or want to just sit and admire the view – take food and water with you, particularly if you have dogs who may get thirsty.

- Respect crops and livestock – keep dogs under control near all animals especially sheep and cattle when their young are with them.

- Respect other people's land and please shut gates behind you.

- Please take all rubbish home with you if you cannot find a litter bin.

- If you are intending to walk on or near beaches, be aware of high and low tides – see following page.

Tides

When walking by the sea it is important to be aware of what the tide is doing. Always check the times of high tide before you set out and know whether it is coming in or going out during your walk. You can find tide times from local radio or in newspapers and many local shops sell tide tables.

The tidal range is much greater at some times than others. Spring tides occur every two weeks around the time of full moon and new moon. The difference between low and high water can be over 5 metres (16ft.) on Cornwall's south coast and 7.5 metres (21ft) on the north coast. Strong on-shore winds can increase the height of tide by up to a metre, especially if accompanied by low atmospheric pressure, usually associated with gales. The time between high and low water is roughly six hours. You are most at risk in the few hours after low water when the tide is returning: it comes in slowly at first but is at its fastest in the 3rd and 4th hours of the flood.

Neap tides, when the range is about half the maximum, occur in the weeks between spring tides. Most tide tables also show the height of high water next to the time – the bigger the number on the day of your walk, the higher the tide will rise.

While we're talking about the sea, just a short word on waves. The complex weather patterns that constantly run into our beautiful Cornish coast often set up wave patterns that cross at an angle to the underlying swell from some distant storm. These will occasionally combine to produce a rogue wave of up to twice the height of the regular waves. There are plenty of clips on-line showing what happens to the reckless when that happens. Don't be one of them!

Below are a few websites you may find helpful.

www.ukho.gov.uk/easytide/EasyTide/ShowPrediction.aspx?PortID=0005&PredictionLength=7
The UK Hydrographic Office is the source of tidal data for all the other sites and limits its free information to the next 7 days.

www.bbc.co.uk/weather/coast_and_sea/tide_tables/10
The BBC list 16 locations around Cornwall and give you a nice little graph of tidal height.

www.newquayweather.com/wxcornishtides.php
Great local weather information. The tides times links you to the UKHO site.

www.cornwalls.co.uk/weather/tide_times.htm
The Cornwall Guide website also provides a wealth of other information for visitors.

www.tidetimes.org.uk/falmouth-tide-times
This site includes an option to order a printed copy of tide tables for the whole year.

WALK ONE
STOWE BARTON
KILKHAMPTON, NEAR BUDE

The starting point for *The Kings General*

Daphne du Maurier wanted to base this novel on the history of Menabilly and the Rashleigh family, so her friend Oenone Rashleigh sent her copies of family letters from the 16th and 17th centuries, a family tree, notes on family members and local history affecting the family.

A. L. Rowse, the eminent Cornish historian, also advised which books to consult to get the history right. While much of the story is based on fact – the characters all took part in the Civil War – the actual love story was of Daphne's imagination, prompted by the discovery that in the 1820s William Rashleigh found the skeleton of a young man walled up inside a buttress at Menabilly. It looked like he was a Cavalier, found sitting on a stool in this tiny room.

Having a vivid imagination, Daphne believed that something ominous had happened to the young man – perhaps he had been murdered. She denied having seen a ghost, but in private she admitted that the Cavalier had stood by the fireplace and smiled at her.

It took Daphne three months to conduct all the necessary research, which she relished. While her household plunged into domestic chaos due to a poorly housekeeper, Daphne locked herself in her room and immersed herself in the 17th century, finishing the novel in July 1945. Her publishers, Victor Gollancz, managed a print run of 75,000 copies, despite paper shortages because of the war, and the book was published in 1946. The history of the book is as follows:

Sir Richard Grenville, of Stowe in Stratton, became famous for fighting 52 Spanish galleons from his own small ship, although he died in the process, becoming a hero of the day. His grandsons, Sir Bevil and Sir Richard Grenville represented both the best and the worst of the Cornish character, Daphne du

Maurier observed. During the Civil War, the Cornish gentry supported the Protestant King, and Sir Bevil and Sir Richard inherited their grandfather's bravery. But the young Richard Grenville inherited his ruthlessness. And it is this brutal streak that runs through *The King's General*, causing his ultimate downfall.

The lovely farmhouse of Stowe Barton stands on the site of the two Grenville homes (for some reason Grenvile is spelled with one 'l' in the book). Across the road are the foundations of the great house built by John Grenville, Bevil's son, over the remains of his father's dwelling when he was created Earl of Bath after the Restoration.

For many centuries the Grenville family were lords of the manor of Kilkhampton but Stowe House was demolished in 1739 and sadly the Grenville family – one of the proudest and most famous of Cornish families – have died out, and nowadays both the Grenville properties are long gone with the old farmhouse at Stowe Barton standing on the remains.

At the beginning of *The King's General*, Honor Harris celebrates her 18th birthday watching a fleet of 80 ships sail into Plymouth Sound, returning from defeat at La Rochelle. There she meets Sir Richard Grenvile, a young Colonel in the King's Army, who has been knighted for extreme gallantry in the field.

Stowe Barton farmhouse

Both sharp tongued and quick witted, the young couple are instantly attracted, despite the ten year difference.

Having met Honor, Richard makes the sudden decision to leave the Army for a while and live at Killigarth, near to Honor's family home of Lanrest, near Looe, while he stands as MP for Fowey. Sir Richard takes to calling on Honor, against the wishes of her brothers, who consider him an ill match for their little sister.

The couple meet regularly in the orchard at Lanrest, and soon fall in love. When another suitor is produced for Honor, and she is told she is to marry him, Honor is distraught and overnight she walks the twelve miles to Killigarth, where Richard is staying, to tell him. Highly amused at her nocturnal wanderings, Richard forbids her to marry this other man, declaring that he wishes to marry her himself, despite his debts and Honor's lack of dowry.

In spite of her family's objections, Honor and Richard become engaged, causing a scandal throughout Devon and Cornwall, and offending many families involved. So Richard's older brother, Bevil, insists that Honor come to Stowe and be married from there, lending an air of approval and decency to the hasty bethrothal.

Although little of the action in the book takes place at Stowe Barton, the pivotal scene in the book, which has the most far reaching consequences, takes place in that location at the beginning of this novel.

One afternoon in May, an afternoon of sport is planned at Stowe, with a banquet that evening. Honor rides a chestnut mare; a present from Richard, and everyone is preparing to go hawking when his sister, Gartred, appears and challenges Richard to a hawk fight. Honor and Gartred dislike each other intensely since her unsuccessful marriage to one of Honor's brothers.

Prior to going out riding, Honor has a premonition of disaster and nearly stays behind, but Gartred taunts her, and so Honor rides out with Richard and Gartred, with brother and sister eager for their hunting birds to compete.

They gallop off, and Honor and her horse follow, excited by the chase. But when Richard warns her of an approaching ditch, she is unable to stop her horse and calls out for help, unsure where the gully is. Gartred ignores her, and Honor and her horse tumble into the deep ditch. As a result, Honor is in

19

a coma for weeks, and when she comes round, finds she is paralysed from the waist down – a condition that afflicts her for the rest of her life.

However, this is far from being the end of the story, as Honor says, "For you will never see me wed to the man I love, nor become the mother of his children. But you will learn that love never faltered, for all its strange vicissitudes, becoming to both of us, in later years, more deep and tender than if we had been wed..."

What you need to know	
Distance	6.5 miles – 7.5 including Duckpool
Allow	At least 4 hours
Suggested Map	OS Explorer 126 Clovelly and Hartland
Starting point	Public car park at Kilkhampton church. Grid reference SS 252113
Terrain	Mostly flat with a few steep hills
Nearest refreshments	London Inn, Kilkhampton, open all day, dog friendly
Public transport	See www.carlberry.co.uk/rfnshowl.asp?L1=KIL0090
Of interest	Stowe Barton farmhouse B&B, Duckpool beach – dog friendly but dangerous for swimming
Facilities	Car park at Kilkhampton, also Duckpool

Directions

One day in late August, Mr B, MollieDog and I arrived at Kilkhampton via the A39, passed the London Inn and parked in the free car park (with toilets) by the side of St James the Great Church. From here we crossed the A39 and turned left, walking past the church, a butcher, the village stores and a few other shops until we came to a little square on the left with a granite memorial erected by the tenants of the Grenville estate. There we turned left behind the church, into West Street.

Walking past rows of cottages down a steep hill, we eventually came to Primrose Cottage on the left, and a public footpath sign on the right leading into Kilkhampton Common. Walking through the kissing gate, we continued downhill and came to a little footbridge over a stream, noting the first fallen beech leaves, and followed the path up into the open common. Soon we came to a junction and took the path up to the right past an information board, and just beyond that we took the permissive path to the right.

Enjoying the abundant blackberries, our hands and mouths were soon stained deep purple. Looking down on the fields below us, we passed sloe bushes bearing dark fruit that made me think I must make sloe gin this year (I never do). The bracken was starting to turn from green to yellowy brown, and we walked along looking down onto the densely wooded Coombe valley ahead. In the distance, a wind turbine stood with silenced arms, and we passed a bench on our right, then some stables before heading downhill past oak trees and a few cabbage white butterflies.

Following another waymark sign, the path led downhill under a canopy of oak trees, and we turned left over a stile by another waymark sign and through a five barred gate. The stony path, with holly bushes on either side, was uneven, slippery and muddy – a river bed, Mr B suggested – as we inhaled the pungent smell of wet earth and wet leaves. The path grew more overgrown and then opened out as we went through a gate at the bottom.

King William's Bridge

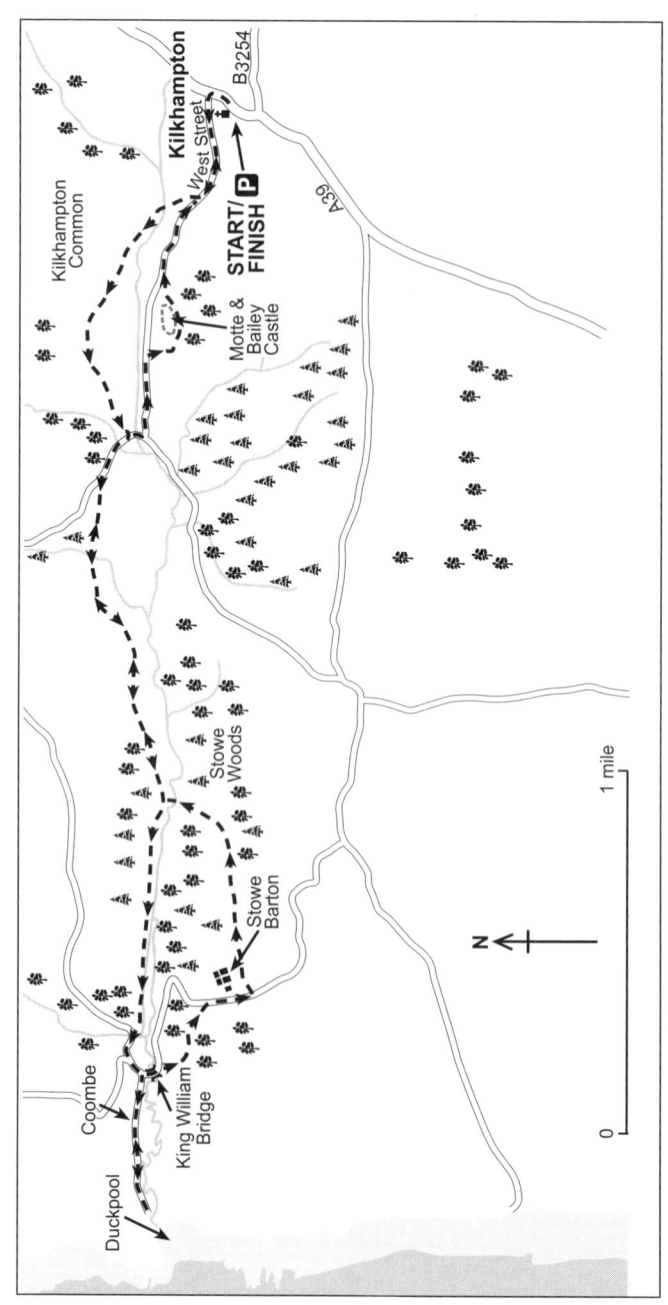

Passing Cross Cottage, and then a small road, we turned right, enjoying the lush countryside. Crossing a little bridge with a pond on the right, we walked past Burridge Farm, with steep hedges of bracken and ivy on either side of this quiet path, while brook thistle grew aplenty in the hedgerows.

Coming to a footpath sign to Canal & Coastpath Duckpool 2.5 miles, near the sign to Sanctuary Farm, we turned right, down a stony track. At this point we were walking along the bottom of the valley with fields on our left and steep beech hedges on our right. Crossing the stream, we walked past an old barn of farm machinery, and came to Sanctuary Farm with staddle stones outside the holiday cottages. Past Orchards Close, we continued downhill then followed a waymark sign through a wooden five barred gate on the right. At a metal gate, with a stream running underneath, we climbed over, following a waymark sign into a field of sheep so we put Moll on the lead.

As we walked along the right hand top side of the field, four black eared sheep watched us intently, still as statues. The densely wooded valley loomed up ahead of us, and we went through another gate into Lee Wood where we noticed a lot of stag beetles, their black bodies gleaming wickedly in the sunshine, while cabbage white butterflies danced round the common toadflax that looked like wild wallflowers.

We walked through another kissing gate and continued through the wood until we came to Mill House, a magnificent, imposing building which looked derelict from the back, but appeared to be inhabited given the cars parked at the front. On our left were fields with reed beds, indicating damp ground at the bottom of Coombe valley.

Walking past Mill House, we came to a small lane with thatched cottages and a ford with a bridge to the side over a river. A perfect, picturesque little hamlet in the middle of nowhere, just as it must have looked several hundred years ago, except for people carrying cleaning materials inside, so they are now probably holiday cottages.

We walked over the bridge, and continued along the minor road, past a garden groaning with apple laden trees – this is a wonderful year for the fruit – which made me think of Richard Grenvile wooing Honor Harris in the orchard at her parent's house near Looe. Few writers would think of trying to seduce their beloved sitting high in the branches of an apple tree.

Hamlet near Mill House

This road led to a junction where we saw another sign indicating Duckpool ¼ mile. This is an addition to the walk, so if you want to do a shorter route, continue the walk over King William's Bridge. However, we followed the road until the valley opened up and we reached Duckpool where Scottish Highland cattle looking like buffalo grazed on a field on our left and the high hedges gave forth the sweetest blackberries, intertwined with the last of the honeysuckle.

Huge cliffs towered over each side of the beach, like steep and forbidding castle walls, while razor sharp rocks dominated the middle of a beach, like a huge dragon's fin. The currents are very dangerous and there is no lifeguard cover either, so do not swim here. A game of rounders was being played when we visited, with dogs running up and down the beach, and there are plenty of rock pools at low tide. Concrete blocks installed in World War II as anti-tank defences are also found here.

The river wanders down the valley until it grows to form a pool, hence the name Duckpool – though we didn't see any ducks – and forms the boundary between the parishes of Morwenstow and Kilkhampton. Peregrines, fulmars and buzzards can be seen around the coast here, while the woods are home to linnets and stonechats.

After a quick sandwich stop, watched by a gulping Moll, eager for the crusts, and a visit to the public toilets, we retraced our steps along the road until we came to King William's Bridge where we turned right. The famous vicar of Morwenstow built this bridge in 1836 part funded by a donation of £20 from King William IV.

Crossing the bridge, we walked along the road until we found a public footpath sign on the right indicating Stowe Barton 0.3 miles, leading uphill through King William Wood. This path was very steep and muddy and the wind rustled noisily in the sycamore trees, but eventually the wood thinned and we could see the satellite dishes on the horizon near Morwenstow, rising like ghostly moons against the scudding clouds.

We went through a couple of kissing gates and continued along a path until we reached a road that led us to Stowe Barton: the farm estate is now owned and let by the National Trust. According to National Trust Heritage records, "Stowe Barton Farm dates from the Post-Medieval period and is an extensive courtyard farm complex close to and incorporating stonework from Stowe Mansion. The complex includes part of the late 17th century H-plan stable block and yard wall. Some buildings from the mansion remain including a cottage further to the east. A real tennis court also survives.

The farm group comprises a farmhouse which incorporates part of the 17th century stable block; a pound house/carpenter's shop wing at the left and rear wing (part stabling). The yard at the rear is partly divided by the rear wing of the house to form smaller yards both of which are sub-divided by low brick walls. The farm buildings ranged around the yards comprise: a single storey lean-to; a single storey gabled store; a gables 2-storey stable range; a cow house/barn range; a calf house with loft and a cartshed.

Standing in the courtyard, I was surprised at how small and friendly the house seemed: framed by elegant old trees, while pots of plants and flowers lined the courtyard walls, and windows were open to the afternoon breeze. It felt like an old friend, waiting patiently for visitors to arrive.

Knocking on the door, we met Angela Flamson who leases Stowe Barton and runs it as a B&B: she is well aware of the importance of the house and land to the local community. "It's lovely that we often get people who have lived or worked here come and knock on the door", she says. "A few times a year there are exhibitions here and they have authors and poets and it comes alive. It would be lovely to see more of that." Angela is always keen to find out more about this house: she and her husband moved here in 2015 when the house was more or less derelict, but they have restored it to a wonderfully gracious, comfortable house.

Walking back along the road, past a beautiful Jacobean wall along the outside of the property, swallows darted overhead, and we saw a sign indicating Stowe Woods 0.6 miles and walked through the field in front of the beautiful long, low farmhouse, which looked much bigger when seen full on. Following the sign down to Stowe Woods we headed downhill into the wooded valley, while far ahead of us, on the skyline, we could see the church of Kilkhampton.

Passing through a kissing gate we went along a stony path while the woods cleared and stonechats sang loudly around us and the river tumbled and splashed to our right. I could just imagine Honor and Richard having trysts here, eager for their imminent wedding day, excited at the prospect of sharing their life together. At a fork in the path we headed right, crossing the stream, and then took a lower path on the left, skirting the woods, with an old settlement up on our right.

As we walked along, the evening sun appeared, highlighting rhododendrons, young oak trees and bracken that was starting to turn brown. The path curved round and over a bridge and soon we found ourselves at the junction we were at earlier, and took the right turn back retracing our footsteps through Lee Wood towards Sanctuary Farm.

Kilk church looked appreciably nearer as we walked back past Burridge Farm and past the turning to Cross Cottage where we walked along the road, crossing over the stream, and at a sign we turned left towards Kilkhampton, up the hill, along a leafy lane, while birds sang overhead. Just past Four Acres house, we took a public footpath sign on the right, through a couple of five barred gates and climbed up a very steep hill to Penstowe, or Kilkhampton Castle.

This motte and two baileys is protected by steep slopes on the north and south sides, and was built between 1066 and the end of the 12th century either by Robert, 1st Earl of Gloucester, the tenant-in-chief of Kilkhampton manor, or by his tenants and relatives of the Grenville family. Kilkhampton would have been quite an important mediæval town and may even have had earlier prehistoric significance; it's thought there may have been a Roman road running through the town on a route that is now the A39.

As we reached the top of the knoll there was a fabulous view back down the deep valley and dark woods all the way to the coast. There was very little sign of human habitation, and I wondered if Richard and Honor had ridden this way – I bet they had, chasing each other on horseback, laughing as they rode.

Mr B was making sheep noises to those in the field to try and get them to pose for a photograph; I don't know what he said, but they scattered pretty quickly. Turning our back on the view, we followed a waymark sign through the trees to the motte (the fort part) and about half way round, found another gate on our right, in between beautiful old oak trees. Going through the gate, via a waymark sign, we found ourselves in a field of cattle, and could see the church over the brow of the hill.

At the far end of the field, we climbed over a stile into a leafy road and turned right. On the opposite bank of the valley we could see people walking over Kilkhampton Common; the route we'd taken on our way out. Climbing upwards we realised this was the steep hill we'd walked down earlier, though it hadn't seemed as steep then. Soon we turned right, back into the square, then turned right to go back to the pub, where Mr B asked the magic question, "Shall we have a drink?"

This is such a stunning, undiscovered part of Cornwall that is well worth exploring. It's rare to walk for so long and not meet any other walkers, yet take in such a diverse landscape – high common ground, wooded valleys, a lovely beach with a duck pond, one of the most beautiful of the old Cornish houses, and a castle earthmound, all in one walk. Richard and Honor may well have ridden along these valleys and lanes, cantered along the beach at Duckpool, and maybe visited the castle. It made me want to read *The King's General* (yet) again and relive the surrounding countryside – and the view from Stowe down to Duckpool is exactly as described in the book.

This novel was dedicated to Daphne's husband, Tommy, "To my husband, also a general, but, I trust, a more discreet one'. Tommy knew that this would make people think that Richard Grenvile was based on him, but he was more amused than upset, though he did hope that it would have a happy ending.

As with many of Du Maurier's novels, this was not the case, but it still remains one of my favourites for a fascinating period of history, remote and wonderful countryside, and at its heart, two strong minded, brave people who loved each other, despite all the obstacles thrown in their path.

WALK TWO

ST NECTAN -
ST NECTAN'S GLEN AND KIEVE

Cornish eccentrics and saints from *Vanishing Cornwall*

The Cornish are renowned for their independence, but this trait can lead to eccentricity – and there have been many eccentrics in Cornwall over the years. Either that, or people had great imaginations.

St Piran arrived at Perranzabuloe, supposedly having been tied to a millstone by pagans and thrown over a cliff. St Ida, the daughter of an Irish chief, apparently arrived in the Hayle estuary on a leaf, and founded St Ives. St Petroc, the son of a Welsh king, arrived via the river Camel and, Moses-style, struck a rock to produce water. After that outstanding feat he lived in poverty near Padstow before travelling east, where he apparently lived for seven years on just one fish.

The martyr St Gennys was exceptional for being able to carry his head in his hands having been beheaded – so the story goes – and St Keyne, who arrived in Cornwall in the seventh century, was known for her ability to turn adders into stones.

Over the years, place names have become muddled with saints and pilgrims. One such example is the rock of Roche. This was supposedly founded by St Roche, of Montpelier in France, who cured people of the plague but then caught it himself. So as not to infect others, he retired to a wood where a dog brought him a loaf of bread every day. There was also another hermit who lived in a cell on the rock nearby and had leprosy. His daughter looked after him and daily brought him water from the nearby well.

The information about St Nectan is confusing, but it appears that he was the eldest son (of 24 children) of King Brychan, a 5th century Celt. All his siblings became saints or martyrs and St Nectan was well loved by the Cornish. He became a monk early on in his life and he and his relatives sailed to North Devon where he lived the life of a hermit by a spring at Stoke, in the forest of Hartland, north of Bude. As St Nectan's Glen is about 30 miles south of Stoke, it's not impossible that he also spent time here, and built a sanctuary, as is suggested.

St Nectan's Glen features a pair of amazing 4,000 year old rock carvings of small mazes known as finger labyrinths. Some says that these tiny carvings, just over an inch wide, are maps of the maze leading to Glastonbury Tor.

The remains of St Nectan's chapel is now a house, beneath which is supposedly where St Nectan lived in his cell. Slate steps lead up to the chapel and the rear bedrock wall forms a natural altar.

In a tall tower high above the waterfall, Nectan apparently kept a small silver bell, and whenever storms occurred, he would ring it to save ships from being wrecked on the rocks below. However, nearing the end of his life, he became convinced that plundering Romans were destroying his religion, so he threw the bell into the basin of the waterfall so that no unbelievers would ever be saved by it again. The saying goes that if the bell rings, it means bad luck is on its way.

Another example of eccentricity occurred near this site. According to Cornish legend, after St Nectan's death, two strange women appeared and took over his cell and chapel. The villagers from Bossiney, the nearest village, knew nothing about these women other than they were well spoken, dignified and kept themselves very much to themselves. They paid for any goods on time, didn't ask any questions and while they had no servant, they never had any visitors, and whenever they went out, they always walked together.

The villagers became suspicious, noting that the women had gathered all St Nectan's chapel vestments, gold and silver and put them in a big chest. They then diverted a stream so they could dig a big hole underneath the original waterfall and there they placed the chest. They then restored the stream and waterfall to their original courses and so his treasures were buried forever.

Word had it that the women whispered to each other in a strange language, possibly to do with the devil. But if the women were witches, there was no evidence: no spells or black cats, and no villagers came to any harm.

Finally word came that one of the women had died, and summoning courage, one of the villagers walked up the valley to find out. There they found one of the ladies distraught and weeping beside her best friend, who was indeed dead.

The remaining woman could not answer any questions or talk about burial: all she could do was cry quietly and persistently. The villagers thought that the body should be removed from the cottage and interred in Christian fashion. Surely this would stir the weeping lady into action?

But it didn't. She let them take the body away, and still she sat there, crying. The villagers left her, thinking that she would realise she needed food, and come to see the grave of her beloved. But nothing happened. For days there was no sign of her, until a bold child peeked through the window and saw the lady sitting in the chair, her handkerchief lying on the floor beside her. She was dead – of a broken heart? The child rushed home and told what she had seen, and the villagers came and collected the dead body, buried it next door to her friend, leaving the mystery of the two ladies still unsolved.

When Daphne du Maurier went to visit the cottage, she found a couple living there, who would show tourists the falls. The wife told Daphne that she was a psychic and could hear footsteps at full moon, knocking at midnight. She was convinced that the ladies were St Nectan's sisters, who came to look after him. They were all buried together, she said, though no bones had ever been found.

However, when Wilkie Collins visited in 1850, and a Mr White in 1854, they were told that the ladies were simply eccentrics who liked a bit of peace and quiet. Nowadays we might assume that they were a couple who just wanted to be together, but knowing that society would frown upon their relationship, kept away from everyone else.

Writers in particular need their peace and quiet, for how else are they to write? Du Maurier particularly needed her solitude and knew she had found this freedom when she first came to Cornwall. As she famously said, "Here was the freedom I desire, freedom to write, to walk, to wander, freedom to climb hills, to pull a boat, to be alone".

In this modern world, particularly, where technology bombards us from every corner, it seems like an excellent idea. Which is why more and more people are taking to walking…

What you need to know	
Distance	4.5 miles
Allow	3 hours to include stop at St Nectan's Glen
Suggested Map	OS Explorer 111 Bude, Boscastle & Tintagel
Starting point	Bossiney car park PL34 0AY; grid reference SX 067889
Terrain	Moderate
Nearest refreshments	Cafe at St Nectan's Glen
Public transport	95 bus from Camelford/Bude
Of interest	St Nectan's Glen, waterfall at St Nectan's Kieve, Neolithic stone carvings at Rocky Valley, St Piran's Well
Facilities	Public toilets at Bossiney car park

Directions

From Wadebridge, Fiona, MollieDog and I took the A39 NE to Camelford, then turned left onto the B3266 then left again onto the B3314 going west for about a mile, before a right turn towards Bossiney on the B3263 on the outskirts of Tintagel. There is a small car park at Bossiney with public toilets and this is the start of the walk.

In the 12th century, a castle was built at Bossiney by Reginald, the illegitimate son of Henry I of England, who made him Earl of Cornwall. Camelot's Round Table is supposed to be buried under the castle ruins and it is said that when King Arthur and his knights are due to return, the Round Table will appear on the eve of the summer solstice.

Bossiney's other claim to fame was that Sir Francis Drake was elected MP for Bossiney in 1584 having given his election speech from Bossiney Mound. But in 1585 war broke out and Sir Drake turned his attention to the Armada.

From the car park at Bossiney, we turned right and headed back the way we'd come, towards Tintagel and then at the Ocean Cove caravan park, we followed a public footpath sign pointing left which leads along a fenced path. We

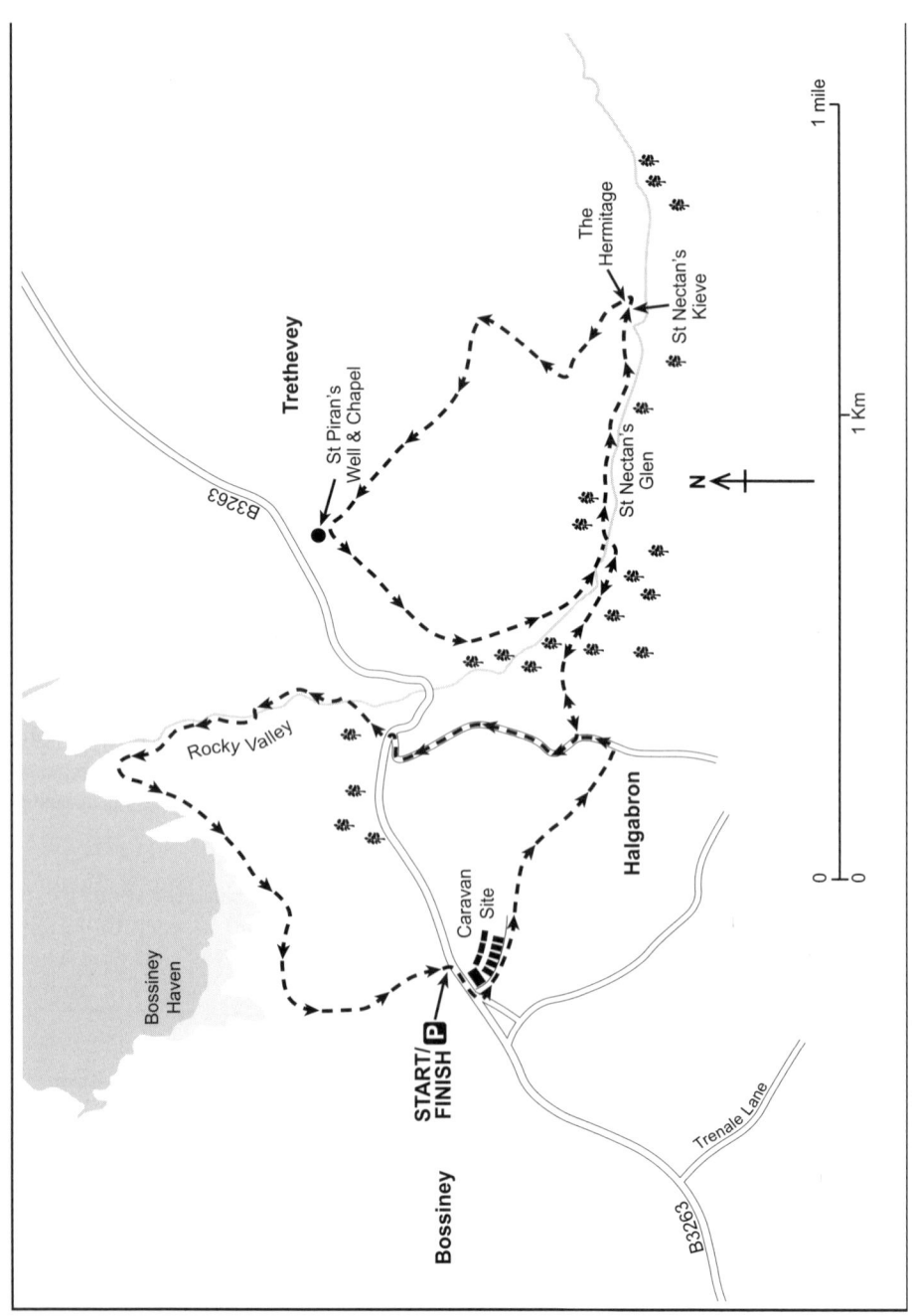

followed this path downhill until we came to a public footpath sign on the right saying Halgabron ¼ mile, Waterfall 1 mile. Walking down some gravelled steps these led to a footbridge over a stream (a tributary of the Trevillet River) and over a stile into a field.

Heading upwards through the field, we aimed for the telegraph pole by a barn and the one to the right of it and found a stile with a cream waymark on the post. It was incredibly quiet here – just the odd blackbird singing, and a stream tinkling in the distance. Climbing over the cantilevered stile, we crossed another field towards another telegraph pole with a stile beside it. From here we followed the right hand hedge to a kissing gate which led into a lane.

Walking down the hill, on a clear day – as it was today – we could see Lundy Island on the horizon to the North. Lundy is the largest island in the Bristol Channel, roughly a third of the way to Wales. It was England's first marine reserve and is owned by the National Trust who rent it to the Landmark Trust. No tarmacked roads, pavements or streetlights are allowed on Lundy and the electricity is turned off at night, giving wonderful views of the inky sky.

Keeping a close eye out for any Cornish eccentrics, we came to a bend in the road with a public footpath sign on the right and crossed over a slate stile into a field. Heading slightly left across the field we came to an iron kissing gate to the right of some farm buildings and followed the path into the woods.

Here bluebells lay in a pale blue haze, intermingled with wild garlic, as we wandered along the path leading through the woods. It was very peaceful here, with the river running down in the valley, far below us, and a robin singing in the sycamore trees. Tendrils of ivy hung from a variety of trees, like dreadlocks – this is how I imagine the Amazon jungle to be (without the bluebells), it's so dense and green here.

At the bottom of the hill we found a footbridge, with a signpost indicating St Nectan's Glen to the right, and St Piran's Well and Trethevy to the left. We turned right and followed the path along the river, leading to another footbridge. From here we continued, along some wooden walkways and eventually a flight of steps leading steadily uphill. It is said that the Cornish folk also walked along this path through the valley, bringing the sick for St Nectan to heal. In our case, we were both well, but it was a longer climb than I'd realised, and by the time we reached the top, and St Nectan's Kieve waterfall and cafe, we were more than ready for our coffee and cake.

A kieve was a wooden tub or basin used for concentrating tin ore. Girls would bash the ore with lump hammers until it became powder and was swirled so that the heavier lumps of ore sank to the bottom, while the lighter particles of unwanted rock could be skimmed off the top.

St Nectan's Kieve was known as Nathan's Cave and was the inspiration for many well known writers and artists at the beginning of the 19th century including the Reverend Hawker and Charles Dickens. Nowadays you can enter and light a candle for your loved ones – which both Fiona and I did.

Many years ago, apparently a group of miners decided to blast the rock away to see if they could find St Nectan's treasure chest. As they were clearing the rock, they suddenly heard a bell ringing and a voice boomed, "The child is not yet born who shall recover this treasure". The miners were so terrified, they hurriedly directed the stream back to its former route and from then on, no one has dared disturb the peace of the Kieve.

The dramatic waterfalls are only accessible on foot, and you have to pay to see them (entrance via the shop near the cafe) where the waters plunge 30 feet, then flow along a narrow channel before diving through another hole and falling 10 feet into a shallow pool.

Having fortified ourselves, we turned left towards the car park and onto a track out of the car park on the left that led over a hill and towards the coast. At the top of the hill, for a nasty moment I thought I'd left our map in the cafe, at the bottom of the steep hill, but thankfully Fiona had tucked it into the second pocket of my rucksack.

We continued along this path, ignoring waymark signs to the right, walking downhill past hedges bursting full of campion, ferns and many bramble flowers, promising a good blackberry year later. Ahead us the sea was a mix of milky green, blue and indigo, with white horse waves whipping the surface – there was a stiff south easterly breeze.

Soon we came to St Piran's Well and chapel at Trethevy. There has been a holy well here for centuries, though the present well was recorded in 1880. Until recently water was drawn by a hand pump at the rear of the building. I particularly like the story that St Piran, patron saint of Cornish miners, is said to have fallen to his death down this well, at the age of 200, after too much to drink.

St Piran's Well

St Piran's Church was first recorded in 1457 when the vicar of Tintagel was granted a licence to celebrate mass here. It's not known when the church went out of use but it's said that a gravestone found built into a house at Trethevy was dated 1707. The church was used as a farm building until 1941 when it was restored for use as a small mission church. Sadly very little of the original church remains.

At a junction by the well and chapel we took a left turn, signposted to the waterfall. Walking downhill, we saw hart's tongue fern, valerian and honeysuckle, as well as some beautiful dog roses rambling in amongst various bushes, their sweet summer smell drifting out as we passed by.

Soon we headed back into the woods with sycamore trees towering overhead. Apparently roe deer can be spotted here, though we weren't fortunate enough to see any. When we came to the footbridge that we arrived at earlier, we retraced our steps through the woods, back through the iron gate and field to the stile where, instead of turning left, the way we'd come, we turned right and headed down a very steep hill.

The hedges were high on either side, one in sunlight and one in the shade, sheltering us from the stiff breeze, and we pondered the vagaries of the Cornish weather: we'd had cold, cloud and wind first thing, then sunshine, rain, and now we were walking in T-shirts and shorts.

Coming to the junction of a fairly busy road (the B3266) we crossed over and took the first right, by a public footpath sign, for Trevillet Mill. Walking down the drive we came to a footbridge, crossed this and followed the path along by the river, which was gushing and tumbling animatedly while we searched for brown trout but to no avail: there was once a trout farm here.

Trevillet Mill manor house was built in 1472 and made famous by Thomas Creswick's painting of *The Valley Mill* which hung in the Royal Academy exhibition of 1851. Passing Trevillet Mill manor and holiday cottages, Fiona said, "how lovely to stay in one of these cottages – imagine lying in bed with the windows open, listening to the river outside. Wouldn't need sleeping tablets, would you?"

Continuing along the winding path strewn with sycamore leaves (it had been very windy recently), the sunlight dappled through the trees, and we crossed over another footbridge so that the river was burbling on our left. We eventually came to the remains of Trevillet Mill which was used in the eighteenth century to manufacture woollen textiles.

Having explored the ruins of the mill, we then crossed over a footbridge and came to a National Trust sign indicating Rocky Valley, and another saying, 'Purchased by funds given in memory of Mary' which made me wonder who she was, and how the hermit St Nectan would feel about having a place named after him?

Beside a waymark sign further on are some labyrinthine carvings on the rockface which could be as old as Bronze Age. This, then, was the famous St Nectan's Glen – and I wondered who had carved these rocks, and whether they really were maps of the maze of Glastobbury Tor? How many people have viewed the carvings since, and pondered their meanings?

Chasm at Rocky Valley

The path winds through this valley with steep rocky cliffs from which elderflower and sycamore grow, while the river rushes and tumbles noisily, like an argumentative child, as if reminding us of the importance of Nature. Rocky Valley has cauldrons, waterfalls and gorges and was formed by running water along a fault line which gives it its steep appearance.

So steep are the cliffs that no animals could graze here, nor houses built, and we didn't see any birds nesting: this valley must have looked very much the same when St Nectan walked along here, seeking solitude. I sincerely hope it stays this way for many hundreds of years to come, with only walkers to appreciate its rough and rugged beauty.

Further along this rocky path, the valley opened out and we came to another footbridge and a steep pile of rocks that we sat on to have a drink of water. We admired the way the stream gathered in a pool before throwing itself into the Atlantic with tremendous force, then was blown up in towering white spumes against the clear blue skies.

From here we turned left and climbed up a steep path with steps up the side of the valley which led to the headland. We stopped at the top to admire the view which was breathtaking: the sea a mixture of milky green and slate, indigo and royal blue flecked with white horses, with the waves pounding and pummelling the rocks beneath us.

Stonechats can be seen in the bushes along here: robin sized little fellows with a black head and orange stomach, and a high pitched chirp that makes them easy to distinguish.

From the headland we followed the path round to the left behind Benoath Cove and, further on, Bossiney Haven. On the far side of the bay is Lye Rock at the end of the headland of Willapark which will soon become a stone stack. It once housed the biggest Puffin colony in Cornwall – in 1948 it was estimated that there were 200 puffins here, but by 1982 they had all died. Nowadays Lye Rock is populated by guillemots and razorbills.

Finally we came to a waymark sign indicating Tintagel straight ahead or Bossiney up the hill. Meeting a couple walking their labrador, they recommended going down to view Bossiney Haven, which we did, but it was in the shade and the tide was in, so no beach was available.

Benoath Cove

So we walked back, up the hill towards Bossiney up a narrow gully, over a field with young cattle (keep dogs on a lead) and finally this led us up a very steep path back to the car park. At the top of the hill here we stopped for a last look back at Lye Rock, at the myriad colours of the living, breathing, tempestuous sea, at the shadows slanting over the coastal path, and although I can quite understand the need for solitude – I need it myself – I would never want to be a hermit.

As we stood, I considered the saints – and eccentrics – who are associated with this walk: St Nectan the hermit. St Piran the 200 year old alcoholic. The 'sisters' in need of some peace and quiet. Who else has retreated to this beautiful part of Cornwall to appreciate the land in peace?

WALK THREE
IN THE SHADOW OF KILMAR TOR
The birthplace of the Merlyn family from *Jamaica Inn*

When 23 year old Mary Yelland's mother is dying, she makes her daughter promise that she will go and live with her Aunt Patience at Bodmin. Broken hearted, Mary is forced to leave the safety of Helford, where she was born and brought up, to go and live with her Aunt Patience and Uncle Joss Merlyn, who she hasn't seen for many years. He is the landlord of Jamaica Inn.

During the journey, Mary begins to realise that strangers turn away from her when they realise she is travelling to Jamaica Inn, and wonders why. Arriving at the Inn after a long, cold and miserable journey, Mary finds that her aunt is now a downtrodden, twitchy shadow of her former self, while her uncle is a bullying giant who, Mary soon finds out, is involved in a major smuggling operation, using the inn as its base for wrecking and murder.

As Mary starts to find out more about what goes on at Jamaica Inn at night, she is by turns horrified and intrigued. The dark inn emphasises the menacing tone of the novel and the surrounding, menacing moorland. Needing to escape in the daytime, Mary begins to explore the moors, and soon learns the different moods of this strange country, so different to the gentle Helford that she is used to. Daphne du Maurier is unrivalled in describing this barren, alien territory that beguiles and terrifies as the wind, sun and rain sweeps across the landscape.

Daphne du Maurier is unrivalled: "To the west of Jamaica high tors raised their heads; some were smooth like downland, and the grass shone yellow under the fitful winter sun; but others were sinister and austere, their peaks crowned with granite and great slabs of stone."

Mary hears wheels stopping outside Jamaica Inn at night, and wonders what they have to do with the barred room at the end of the passage, but when she asks her aunt, the older woman warns her off, telling her that evil things happen at the inn. She tells Mary that she must lie in bed and put her fingers in her ears. And never question anyone or Mary would age and grey just as her aunt has done.

Seeing how much she has upset her aunt, Mary asks no more but begins to acquaint herself with her household duties, which still leaves plenty of time for exploring. Wandering over the moors, Mary meets her uncle's younger brother, Jem, who earns his living as a horse thief. A better looking version of his brother, Jem tells her that his cottage is across the Withy Brook, the other side of Trewartha Marsh, at the foot of Twelve Men's Moor. Mary finds herself there one day, and calls on him. Despite not trusting him, he is much less brutal than his brother and she finds it hard to resist his charm and sense of humour. He is as enigmatic as he is independent, and therefore a good match for Mary, and their lives start to cross at unexpected points throughout the book.

Mary determines not to be cowed into submission by her uncle, who admires her spirit, and occasionally confides in her. At the beginning of the book, he tells her about where the Merlyn brothers were born, not far away, on Twelve Men's Moor.

"I'm the eldest of three brothers, all of us born under the shadow of Kilmar, away yonder over Twelve Men's Moor. You walk out over there across the East Moor till you come to Rushyford, and you'll see a great crag of granite like a devil's hand sticking up into the sky. That's Kilmar. If you'd been been under its shadow you'd take to drink, same as I did."

The name 'Twelve Men's Moor' supposedly came about when the moorland, owned by Henry, the Prior of Launceston, was divided up between twelve tenants in 1284 at a rent of four silver shillings a year, to be paid at Michaelmas. In return for the privilege of being tenants, they had to pay homage and service. The twelve men's farmland was spaced out with the right of pasture over it. It was a hard life for moorland farmers who needed more staying power than the farmers in the valley to survive, let alone make a living.

The moors are the constant backdrop for this novel, which weaves together murder, thieving, wrecking, subterfuge and many a clash of minds and wit. The landscape offers no protection or sympathy for the inhabitants of Jamaica Inn and it is impossible to think of the lonely, isolated Inn without imagining

Bodmin Moor in all its terrifying glory. While Cornwall's weather – and mood – can change in an instant, here on the moors the changeability is magnified, from a place of raw and ancient beauty, to one of terror – the perfect place for murder.

What you need to know	
Distance	4 miles
Allow	2½ hours
Suggested Map	OS Explorer 109 Bodmin Moor
Starting point	Layby; grid reference SX 258758
Terrain	Rugged moorland, bogs, wear suitable footwear
Nearest refreshments	Fat Frog Cafe, 6 Market St, Liskeard PL14 3JJ – dog friendly and excellent food
Public transport	None
Of interest	Kilmar Tor, Trewortha Tor, King Arthur's Bed, numerous quarries and settlements, hut circles and standing stones
Facilities	None

NOTE: It is advisable to do this walk when it has been dry for a while as moorland can be extremely boggy and dangerous. Suitable footwear is vital as the ground can be rocky and wet. This walk is suitable for able bodied walkers only.

Directions

From the A30 Viv, MollieDog and I headed east one bright Sunday morning in early October, taking the B3257 turning after Altarnun. We continued until Congdon's Shop where we turned right, and this led to Berriowbridge where there was a large B&B on the left over the river Lynher. After the bridge, we turned sharp right, along an unsigned, narrow No Through Road, which climbed steeply and continually uphill. We continued until we reached the moor and parked in a layby on the right with room for half a dozen cars.

From here we followed a public bridleway sign past a sign advising that dogs should be kept on a lead between the 1st March and 31st July. Heading over a cattle grid we found ourselves on Twelve Men's Moor, whose vast, majestic landscape stretched in every direction like an alien planet. Ahead of us was the long ridge of Kilmar Tor, while on our right was Trewortha Tor and behind that, King Arthur's Bed.

The sun peeped out to welcome us as we strode off over the moor, in the footsteps of Mary Yelland, to where the Merlyn brothers were born. We bore left on the grassy track, with a stone wall on our left, over rough and springy turf interspersed with reeds, while the dogs leapt and bounced in front of us. Stunted, gnarled gorse trees greeted us as we walked past, their twisted branches bending backwards like arthritic arms: it was easy to imagine their spookiness on a misty, cold winter's day.

"You'd have to be hard to live here", said Viv, as we stared at the tors around us, towering against the sky. "There must be a different breed of people." As indeed the Merlyns were.

Sheep and cattle grazed on this ground which has open access, so please be careful with dogs – we put ours on leads as soon as we saw livestock: the

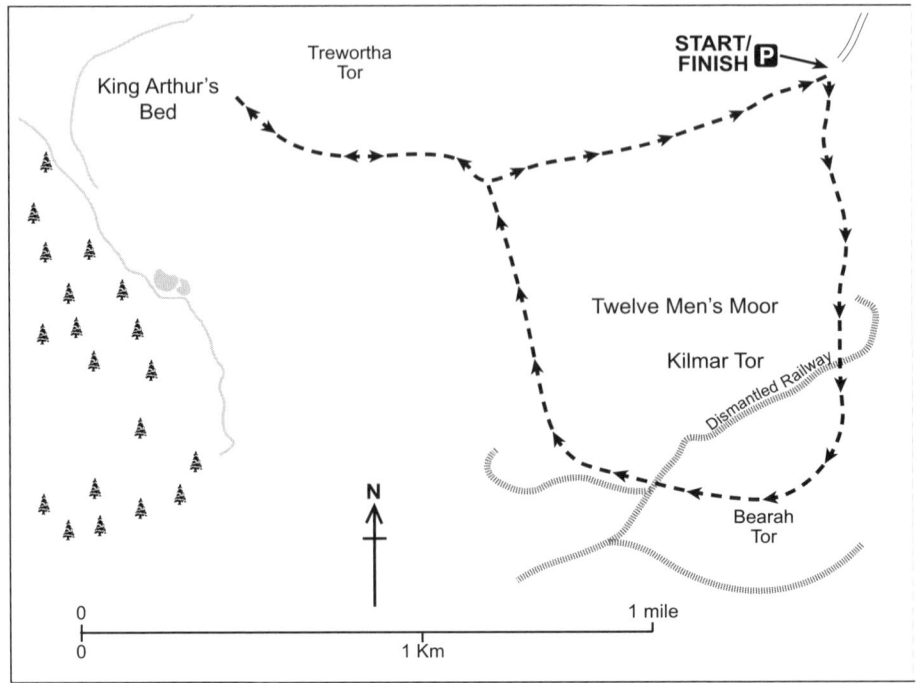

Ponies on Twelve Men's Moor

sheep tended to scuttle away in fright, whereas the cattle just stared at us, rather ominously.

When the wall curved round to the left, we continued walking straight ahead – there is no direct path here, but it's easy to pick your way through the moorland, heading towards the ridge that extends left of Kilmar Tor. Climbing upwards, we eventually reached an old cart track where we turned left and reached the top of the ridge.

From here we continued left, heading for the least rocky part of the Bearah ridge, past a small, disused quarry. There are magnificent views over Twelve Men's Moor – the long ridge of Bearah Tor in front of us, with Sharp Tor behind it, and Kilmar Tor on our right – at 1,280 feet, the highest tor around here. A stone quarry is still in use on the far side of Kilmar Tor, and the sheer breadth and depth of this moorland is awe inspiring, almost like a desert stretching into infinity, surrounded by tors of all descriptions. Some were in shadow, some lit by the sun, and suddenly the moorland stopped, and there were fields on either side, making us wonder if the moor was some strange trick of the eye.

"This place makes you feel very insignificant", said Viv, as we looked over the ancient landscape, with evidence of stone circles, burial chambers, standing stones and settlements. "It's all been here long before us, and will be so long after us."

There are various boggy parts of the moor so be very careful – this was how Matthew Merlyn drowned, as Mary Yelland so vividly imagines … "In her fancy …. before he had taken five steps he felt the ground sag under his feet, and he stumbled, and fell, and suddenly he was up above his knees in weed and slime. He kicked once more, and one foot sucked itself free, but, as he plunged forward, reckless and panic stricken, he trod deeper water still, and now he floundered helplessly, beating the weed with his hands. She heard him scream in terror, and a curlew rose from the marsh in front of him, flapping his wings and whistling his mournful cry."

Path up to Kilmarth Tor

We didn't see many birds on our walk, but golden plover feed on the moorland here. Also, this area is the last site of the Cornish path moss as well as many other lichens, mosses and liverworts.

Cornish bladderseed is found on the stony slope woodlands and scrub of Bodmin Moor, and the marsh fritillary butterfly feeds on Devil's-bit scabious, which is found in valleys and damp grassland areas.

Otter and salmon can be found in the rivers here, and a variety of bats, including the rare greater and lesser horseshoe species breed, roost and feed on these Moors.

From our viewpoint, we retraced our steps for 50m and headed for the far left end of Kilmar Tor, passing an old, smaller, disused quarry. After about 750m we came across the trackbed of the old Kilmar Railway which was built to carry granite from the quarries here down to Looe, and closed in 1882.

"We should really have a compass", said Viv, knowing my navigational abilities of old. I do have one but it's sitting at home and I've never quite got the hang of compasses, though this is probably not the time nor place to admit to such a failure.

Walking through the lower part of the moor is an eerie, bleak and chilling land. The tors, surrounding us on the high ground, now seemed to have receded into the distance and their presence was somehow comforting, giving points of reference. Without them we seemed abandoned, and it was extremely disconcerting. Even if we weren't actually lost, for once.

It turns out there are several railway trackbeds leading round Kilmar Tor – we eventually found the lower one but we should have aimed for the higher one, which skirts the bottom of the tor. These are raised beds, with the remains of granite sleepers, which we shared with cattle and ponies who stared at us with interest.

Kilmar Tor

We followed the trackbed round the edge of the Kilmar ridge, and where it peters out, we turned left down a very steep, rocky path more suitable for goats than humans, and clambered over granite boulders, reeds, gorse and boggy ground littered with rabbit and horse droppings. Over on our left, we noticed Smallacoombe Plantations, an area of pine forest that ended so sharply it looked as it it had been sliced, like a cake. Further away, Siblyback Lake (reservoir) glimmered in the distance.

From here we continued walking north towards Trewortha Tor and the flat topped tor of King Arthur's Bed, towards the long curved wall that encircles it. Within this wall the ground was dotted with pale blue blobs that from a distance looked like small hay bales, or frozen sheep. "Perhaps they're in shock", said Viv helpfully, though as we grew nearer, these blobs started moving – it transpired that their fleece had been dyed blue – to prevent poaching?

Eventually, nearing the wall, we came to a metalled track leading to Trewortha Farm. We crossed over this, passed through a gate and headed up towards King Arthur's Bed as the sun came out and the afternoon sun cast long golden shadows over the rough ground, illuminating some wonderful circular thistle heads.

Returning to the metalled track, we turned left and continued along here until we arrived back at the layby where we'd parked the car. "We didn't get lost", said Viv in amazement. "Who needs a compass? Look – I've still got my emergency banana."

While this landscape can be threatening, it is also Mary Yelland's friend, for it provides her with a means of escape. She decides she will stay at Jamaica Inn until the spring and hope to persuade her aunt to run away with her and return to the Helford valley. In the meantime, Mary makes the most of her time exploring, finding out more about her uncle and his colleagues, and what they really get up to. Her bravery is accentuated by the starkness of the landscape, which is very masculine and bare in contrast. The loneliness of the moors seeps through the novel, becoming the fear and isolation that Mary herself feels.

This magnificent landscape really does make you appreciate the grandeur of nature – the tors loomed over us like somnolent lions, chuckling at the stupidity of mankind, but, I felt in a kindly way. On wintry days when the

Windswept tree leading up to King Arthur's Bed

moorland mist descends, this landscape is another world altogether. Enjoy the moorland but always, like the sea, retain a firm respect for it. It has no compassion for carelessness, as Matthew Merlyn found to his cost.

WALK FOUR
ALTARNUN

From *Jamaica Inn*
The Inny Valleys walk of many stiles

The name Jamaica Inn goes back to 1789: it is thought that the inn sold Jamaican rum, but the Cornish historian H. L. Dutch thought it was a sarcastic comment made because the area is so unlike Jamaica.

Daphne was amazed by the moors, so different from the coast and valleys of Helford and Fowey. "I came unprepared for its dark, diabolic beauty", she writes in *Daphne du Maurier's Cornwall*. "When I first set eyes on the old, granite faced inn itself it made me think that there was a story there, peopled with moorland folk in strange harmony with their background."

Daphne had the idea for the novel when she was out riding with her close friend, Foy Quiller-Couch, on Bodmin Moor, and visited Jamaica Inn. She was influenced by *Treasure Island*, which she was reading at the time, and started thinking of using the inn as a centre for wrecking and smuggling. She then met the white haired vicar of Altarnun and so the story started to take shape.

Daphne and Foy set off over the moors on what should have been a forty minute ride. But the track disappeared into a stream which swiftly became a torrent as storm clouds gathered, blocking out the sun and suddenly Bodmin Moor became a place of danger, of horror. Daphne and Foy rode round in circles before sheltering in a derelict cottage. When her heroine Mary also becomes lost on the moors, Daphne uses her own experience to describe Mary's sense of isolation, of desolation at her hostile surroundings that seem to stretch for mile after mile of bogs, craggy tors and evil marshland. Somewhere in all this was the main road to Bodmin, and Jamaica Inn. But where?

It is at this point in the story that Mary meets Francis Davey, the albino vicar of Altarnun. She is lost, lonely and frightened, and comes across this lone rider who speaks with a low and gentle voice. He seems "a person of quality" so she feels she can trust him. But then she sees his strange, transparent eyes: "a freak of nature and a freak in time" as he describes himself, with a halo of cropped white hair and a prominent thin nose. "Crouched in his seat, with his black cape coat blown out by the wind, his arms were like wings.'"He looks like a sinister bird, but when he smiles at Mary, he seems human again.

The vicar initially seems a man at peace with himself – and, presumably, God. But later on, Mary glimpses a picture he has painted of Dozmary Pool on a grey day and is disturbed by its malevolent power. He feeds Mary supper in silence, but when he asks what she was doing, lost on the moors, his soft persuasive voice calms her and she feels she can trust him. So she tells him how frightened she is by what she has seen happening at Jamaica Inn: wagons being moved, the abuse of her aunt, how she believes a man was murdered. He is calm, listens in silence and tells her that she is always welcome at Altarnun, and if anything else frightening happens she is to come and tell him about it.

Reassured, Mary allows him to take her back to Jamaica Inn, but she sees another side to the vicar: this time he rides a big, fast grey cob, and constantly urges his steed to go faster in a voice that is low and excited; unlike his voice at the vicarage. And then the moment passes, and he is back to being the strange freak of nature who claims to be her friend.

Altarnun

At each encounter with the vicar there is an undercurrent of his sexual interest in Mary but it never comes to anything: rather it runs alongside like a sinister soundtrack, threatening and persistent.

It is not until nearing the end of the story, when Mary's uncle and aunt are dead and she is taken to the vicarage that Francis Davey's true self comes to light. He is the ringleader of all this violence and plundering: the clever mastermind behind it all who uses the Cornishmen as pawns to do his work. The vicar admits that, like other Du Maurier's characters, he feels he has come from ages past, "when the rivers and the sea were one, and the old gods walked the hills". Yet despite his outward appearances, he is very far from God.

"Sometimes the wind shouted and cried, and the cry echoed in the crevices, and moaned, and was lost again ... there was a stillness in the air and a stranger, older peace, that was not the peace of God."

These moors do carry this very sense of the ancient with them, and the views of both coasts are amazing in good weather. I feel the ancient splendour and invisible dangers every time I walk here, so it's easy to imagine Francis Davey in such a setting: he is in perfect harmony with the treacherous moorland, yet the benign, beautiful setting of Altarnun is a perfect contrast to his 'diabolical' nature.

What you need to know	
Distance	5 miles
Allow	2½-3 hours
Suggested Map	OS Explorer 109 Bodmin Moor
Starting point	Altarnun Street; grid reference SX 223813
Terrain	Hilly in parts, a lot of stiles
Nearest refreshments	The Rising Sun Inn www.therisingsuninn.co.uk/about-us
Public transport	425 bus from Launceston
Of interest	St Nonna Church, Laneast Church, Gimbletts Mill
Facilities	None at time of walking

Directions

From Bodmin, take the A30 NE, then turn left at the Trewint/Five Lanes/Altarnun exit and follow the signs to Altarnun. This quietly beautiful village lies in the sheltered valley of Penpont Water, which is a tributary of the River Inny, named in the Domesday Book as Penpont. The village shop was once the Ring O'Bells pub, and next door is an 18th century Methodist chapel, with a carved head of John Wesley over the door. The local craftsman, Nevil Northey Burnard, famous not only for this head of Wesley but for sculpting the head of Edward VII, Prince of Wales and Duke of Cornwall.

'Altarnun' is actually incorrect: the spelling should be Altarnon, meaning the altar of St Non, or Nonna, who was the mother of St David and gave the church its name. St Nonna's altar was preserved at this church and it is believed that Celtic Saints would carry this altar with them. The Norman church was built in the 12th century from unquarried stone from the moors, then added to in the 15th century using stone from the Trelawney family mansion when the family left the area.

There is a Holy Well nearby into which the lunatics of the area were thrown, in the belief that a sharp shock would cure them of their madness.

Driving into the village one sunny afternoon in May, Mr B, MollieDog and I parked in the street near the church, crossed the 15th century packhorse bridge and walked up the lane, past the church. The Old Rectory, built in 1842, was visited by Daphne du Maurier and features as the home of Francis Davey.

Continuing up past huge pine trees with pale green fingertips of new growth, we were accompanied by bouquets of wild garlic growing in the hedges. Passing the Travellers' Rest campsite on the right, we headed up the hill towards Camelford. The last of the bluebells scented our way as we continued up the steep hill, with very tall hedges on either side covered in a duvet of the longest fronds of emerald moss I've ever seen. The road was evidently hewn out of slabs of slate, in and out of which wound gnarled tree roots, like an Aubrey Beardsley drawing.

Coming to Treween, we turned right past a very ancient Celtic Cross in the hedge, so old we could hardly make out the carving. We headed down a narrow lane, past Rose Park on the right – a beautiful fishing park – and at the top of the hill we noted a public footpath sign on our right, but ignored that and turned slightly to the left where we took the first public footpath

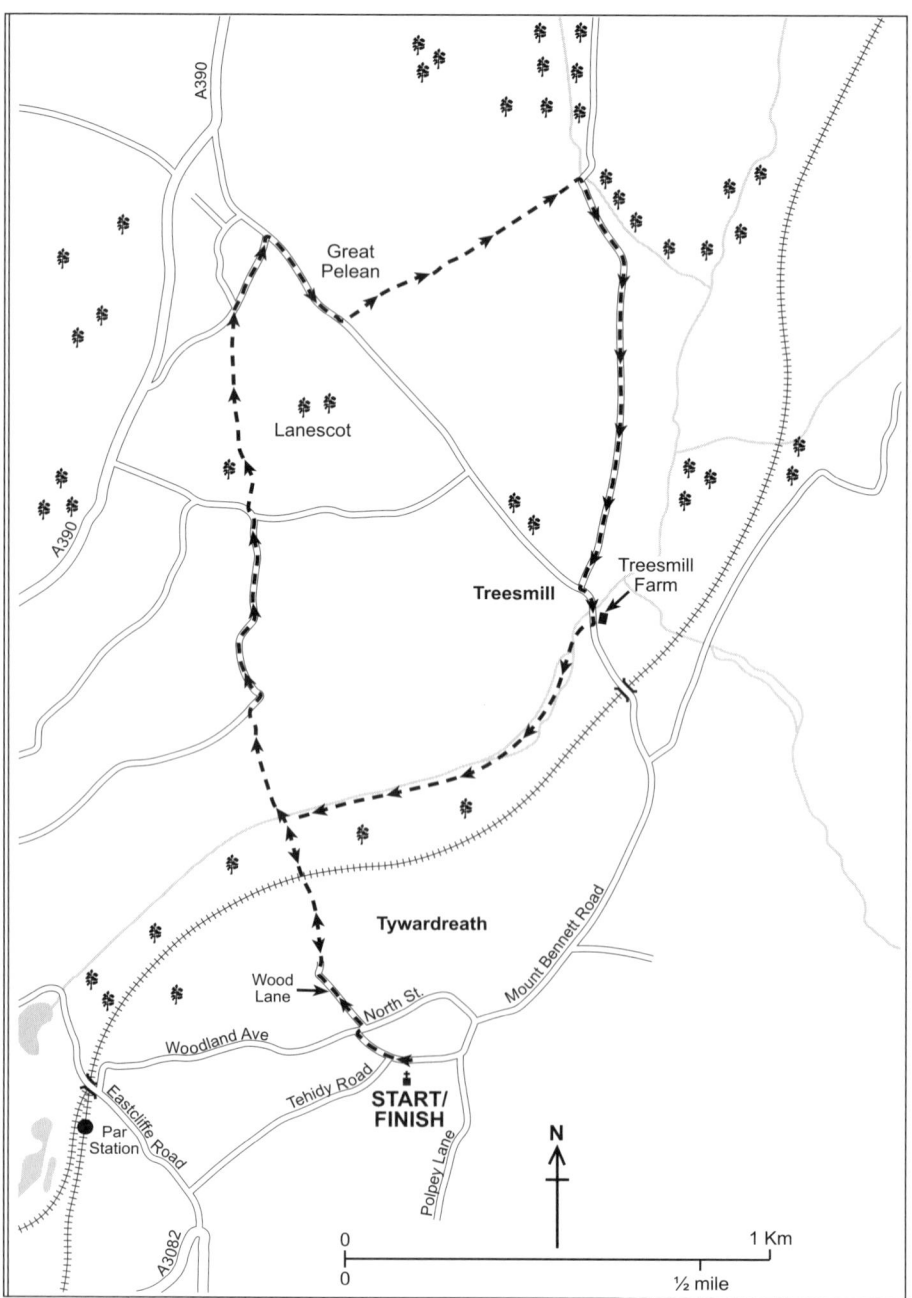

sign over a tall hedge and into a large field of long grass dotted with celandines and cuckoo flower, or ladies' smock.

Walking through the middle of the field, we came to a big granite stile a third of the way along the opposite hedge into a copse. Here we found a path meandering through the young oak trees, as well as ash and beech, while birds sang loudly in the sunshine. We crossed an old narrow lane and climbed over another stile into a field full of sheep.

At this time of year, when lambs are in abundance it is, of course, necessary to keep dogs on leads. We headed over the middle of this field, admiring the adorable lambs, some of them black and fluffy, guarded by worried looking mums, and at the far end, had to climb over a wire fence in order to get over the next stile, then over another stile into another field of sheep.

Grarled oak roots

Aiming for the right hand hedge with a hole in it, with gorse flower shining brilliantly through it, we made our way through more sheep, dodging a particularly angry looking ram, until we reached another stile and field and a wooden stile. Looking over our shoulder was the most wonderful view – a patchwork of fields in varying shades of green, East Moor in its sunlit glory, and a wonderful collection of trees of all kinds of shape, colour and sizes. Ahead of us, the sun lit up a bright red rhododendron tree with yellow gorse bushes underneath it and a turbine, blades turning lazily in the sultry afternoon.

Climbing over another stile by a beech tree we found a public footpath sign opposite, by Higher Tregunnen Farm on the right, and the most beautiful old

53

chestnut tree. We walked through the farm yard while the farm's collie approached us and Mr B gave me instructions on what to do if a dog goes for you – you must get your back against the wall, apparently.

The collie proved friendly, however, if persistent in his unrequited admiration of Moll, and we walked through the farmyard and found a waymark sign pointing left (on a pole on a barn on the right). This led into a field which we headed straight across, noting some hot looking sheep sheltering in the shade of an old oak tree, while the hedges were full of golden gorse.

This next stile led into a field of cows, of which I am always wary, but we managed to get through unscathed, noting the church tower of St Clether peeping out over the trees on our left. The next stile, half way down a hedge, was particularly tall and awkward, but we emerged into a path through the gorse. Over another stile and down some wooden steps, we found ourselves on a very ancient track and followed the waymark sign straight ahead.

This path was very steep and winding: we were glad to be heading down rather than up, while the celandines sprang from the grass like little yellow stars. We could see the river Inny at the bottom of the valley as we waded through a boggy part, and we wondered how many people had ever done this walk before: there were no foot, paw or hoofprints, and it was so beautiful and unspoilt.

Over another wooden stile, down some slate steps, we arrived in a road and turned right. Further along, we came to a bridge and walked over the River Inny, revelling in the quiet beauty of the countryside – so different from the wildness of the moors a few miles away. Mary Yellan may well have walked these paths when exploring, to get away from her uncle Joss, and would have found a quietness to soothe her soul along these lanes.

Peering into the river, we spotted a few tiny brown trout swimming in the water which was wide but not deep, and Mr B decided to do a spot of gold panning. I had a rest in the sun and enjoyed watching the river, as it burbled and rushed over stones of a deep red. After about twenty minutes, with no sign of any gold, Mr B looked up, slightly crestfallen. "I think we've got the wrong spot", he said.

We continued over the bridge and up the hill, admiring the tranquil valley, the sheep spotted black and white against the emerald grass, the elegant oak trees framed against a brilliant blue sky. As we climbed, we noted a lower path along by the river, with wild iris growing alongside.

Climbing further still we came to a few cottages with a stone cat outside, and quince growing up the outside of the house, its red flowers brilliant against the whitewashed walls. At the top of the hill we noted a church on our left and a village noticeboard confirmed we were in Laneast.

'Lan' originally meant 'monastery' in Cornish, but came to mean 'church', and this one, at the head of this wooded valley, was originally a chapel established by the Augustinian priory at Launceston. Inside the church is a black marble plaque in memory of the famous Cambridge University astronomer John Couch Adams, who discovered the planet Neptune. He was born at Lidcott, within the parish, and died in 1892. John Wesley, the founder of Methodism, is said to have preached from the Laneast pulpit six times, and very much enjoyed it.

Meandering through the sunny village it felt more like summer, listening to the distant drone of a lawnmower. Coming to a junction at Holywell Place, we followed a public footpath sign on our right which led through another farm. The path was diverted from the farmyard via a stile over a concrete wall, into a narrow lane then out via another stile and down into a grassy area, to another stile into a field with two gorgeous horses grazing.

From here we headed down the right hand side of the field until we came to a waymark sign at the next gate and walked down the hill towards a telegraph pole – it was more like walking through parkland rather than farmland here, the fields are so big and majestic, with oak and beech trees towering over the grass.

At the bottom, by a big oak tree, we crossed stone slabs over a stream which led to a stile and into another field. We turned right then found another stile where we walked through long grass towards Treroose Farm. Here we stopped, suddenly, as two deer ran right in front of us – an amazing sight that left me quite shaken. Walking past magnificent old beech trees and farm buildings on our right, it seemed almost as if we'd arrived in another part of England. None of this looked very Cornish.

Coming to a very ancient stile with a waymark sign pointing left, we walked onward and found a stile on the right into another field where we walked

Bridge by Gimbletts Mill

along the right hand side before resting in the shade of an oak tree for a snack and a drink. At the end of this field is a stile with a waymark sign pointing left and further on, we found another waymark sign.

Heading along a rough track, we came to a metal gate leading to a lane and turned right, with farm buildings on the left named Trespean Barns with swallows swooping and diving, jackdaws flying overhead, and a group of conifers on our right. Walking down a leafy lane underneath a canopy of sycamores, we came to a bend on the right and paused to admire the view over a field with a huge oak tree with stones at the base of its trunk. Continuing along the lane, we descended into the valley with a cock crowing in the distance, until at the bottom we came to Gimbletts Mill, a beautiful flour mill dating back to around 1650, that was in production until the 1950s.

Leaving this idyllic spot behind, we crossed over the bridge and headed up the road the other side on what promised to be a long, hot haul, given how far we'd walked down. Still, the hedges were stunning with their spring array of pink, white, blue and yellow – campion, stitchwort, bluebells and buttercups. Ignoring the public footpath sign at the first bend (this would be the Inny Valleys walk), we continued uphill looking out over dense woods – unusual for Cornwall – with all kind of trees: ash, oak, beech and sycamore in various stages of growth and colour. Past Landinner Farm, the road continued up and round, past Lower Tregunnon Farm until we came to a junction with a letterbox in the barn opposite and a sign indicating Altarnun straight over, so we walked down there. Soon we found a stile in a hedge on the right into a field of sheep.

From here we crossed several fields and stiles, heading towards the middle of the fields. The stiles aren't always easy to find, with one in the left hand corner of the field, but with careful perseverance, and climbing over a wire fence into another field of anxious sheep, we came to a wooden stile on the left and steps leading down into a lane. We headed straight up the narrow lane and found a public footpath sign on our right over a stile into another field. Half way down the opposite hedge we found an old waymark sign underneath a pussy willow tree, and ended up in a field. Walking diagonally left to the next stile, this led to the road where we had walked up nearly three hours earlier.

From here we walked down the road and back into Altarnun. By this time it was 5pm and the village was bathed in mellow afternoon sunlight, looking utterly magical. I wanted to see if I could find any trace of my Kittow ancestors in the church, so we walked into the churchyard to hear the organ playing. Evensong, I thought, and left Mr B holding Moll outside while I crept into the church. No service was taking place, but there was much hive and bustle, and a very friendly fellow who showed me a brass plaque saying "To the glory of God, 1913, given by John Kittow" – he had apparently given the pulpit to the church.

On that happy note, we sat by the bridge enjoying the last of the sun before heading back home over the moors. I hadn't thought that a walk so near the moors would be so secluded, so peaceful and stunning – I would love to do it again. On such a beautiful day it was difficult to imagine such a devious, dangerous man as Francis Davey in this peaceful, sunlit village – which, of course, is why the Vicar of Altarnun is such a brilliantly clever villain.

WALK FIVE
LANTEGLOS CHURCH AND THE HALL WALK
One of Daphne's regular walks, including the church where she married

Fowey lies at the end of the Saints' Way from Padstow and can be reached by a car ferry from the hamlet of Bodinnick, near the Du Maurier's house, Ferryside. There is also a passenger ferry between Fowey and Polruan, though the normal approach by car is via the A390, turning off between St Austell and Fowey. Fowey was established as a town in 1300 because its natural harbour encouraged trade with Europe, and local ship owners would often hire out vessels to the king to support various wars. Piracy was also prevalent at this time.

In the 14th century blockhouses were built on each side of the harbour entrance, but these were unable to prevent the French attacking in 1457. On St Catherine's Point a small castle was built in 1540 from where soldiers beat off a Dutch attack in 1667.

Hall, the home of the Mohun family, was built in the 13th century just above Bodinnick, and was once the most important manor in the area. The Hall Walk, created in 1585, is an early example of a private ornamental promenade. Part of its terraced gardens, which zig-zagged down the hillside to the river, were leased by Sir Arthur Quiller-Couch in the early 1900s. The walk was given to the National Trust as a joint memorial to those who died in the Second World War, and to Sir Arthur Quiller-Couch, whose novel *Troy Town* featured the area.

The Du Maurier family first visited Fowey from London, and Daphne was instantly captivated by what she perceived as "a gateway to another world", having travelled from Looe to Bodinnick. Climbing up the hill by the Old Ferry Inn, they noticed a house built overhanging the water, like a chalet, named Swiss Cottage. An old boat shed and sail loft, it was several storeys high – and it was for sale.

The Du Mauriers were looking for a holiday house, and Daphne instantly fell in love with Swiss Cottage. To her joy, her parents bought, refurbished and renamed the house Ferryside. On May 14th, 1927, the day after Daphne's twentieth birthday, she had the best birthday present of all: to be left alone there for the first time in her life.

Happier than she had ever been, Daphne embraced Cornish life, travelling back and forth on the Bodinnick ferry (in those days rowed by a ferryman), getting to know the locals and burying herself in books on Cornish history. She became friendly with the seamen and listened to their stories, and in particular made friends with a boatman named Adams who taught her how to sail, how to fish and go rabbiting. Having written various short stories in London, she was determined to start writing seriously.

On one of her many rambles on the Hall Walk, around Pont Creek, she found a derelict schooner called the *Jane Slade*. The poor boat lay rotting in the mud while the elegant figurehead protruded proudly, reminiscent of her days at sea. Daphne was fascinated by the boat, and discovered from Adams that the figurehead was of Jane Slade, his wife's grandmother, and the mother of the boatbuilders who had built the boat at Polruan.

Bodinnick side of River Fowey

Adams asked if Daphne would like the figurehead. Delighted, she agreed, and so it came to live on a beam outside her bedroom window at Ferryside. She became so fascinated by the Slade family that she read all the old family letters Adams gave her, and discovered Jane had been married and was also buried at St Wyllow (Lanteglos church), alongside her husband, Christopher. As Daphne read, and explored Fowey, so the beginnings of a novel came to her. This was to be *The Loving Spirit*, based on Jane Slade's life.

Once she started writing, Daphne worked hard, and in two weeks she had written 45,000 words. Part Two followed in another three weeks, before she got stuck on the history. Thankfully a local man lent her more books about life at the turn of the century, so that she was able to complete Part Three. Christmas interrupted her writing, but in January 1928 she locked herself away, battling her lack of confidence. She was optimistic about her portrayal of the main character, who was similar to Daphne in her wish to have been born a man. Unsure of the book's reception, she sent it off to Michael Joseph who loved it. When Heinemann said they would publish it with minor revisions, Daphne was delighted. Once the book was published, this gave Daphne sufficient confidence and encouragement in her abilities as a writer to take her work seriously.

Gravestones at Lanteglos church

One of the fans of *The Loving Spirit* was 35 year old Major Tommy Browning, the youngest major in the British army and known as Boy to his friends, as he looked so much younger than his 35 years. He was so impressed by the book, and the descriptions of Fowey, that he decided to go and see the place for himself, so he and a friend sailed Tommy's boat down the coast to Fowey and cruised up and down the harbour, where he was instantly spotted by Angela, one of Daphne's sisters. However, he made no attempt to contact the Du Mauriers just then.

The following year, Daphne was in Fowey recovering from appendicitis when she heard that Major Browning was back afloat and would like to meet her. He took her out on his boat and from then on they spent as much time together as possible. She was impressed by his good looks, his maturity and discipline, high standards, and the fact that they both loved the same things. Two months later they were engaged, but it was Daphne who proposed.

What you need to know	
Distance	4 miles
Allow	2½ hours
Suggested Map	OS Explorer 107 Austell & Liskeard
Starting point	Fowey main car park; grid reference SX 122517
Terrain	Some steep hills, can be muddy
Nearest refreshments	The Old Ferry Inn, Bodinnick, Pinky Murphy's Cafe, Fowey and many other pubs and cafes in Fowey
Public transport	Nearest station: Par or St Austell. Bus: 24/25. Polruan ferry, Bodinnick ferry (to Looe); Polruan ferry £2 each plus 40p per dog. Bodinnick ferry £1.80 on foot www.ctomsandson.co.uk Fowey to Mevagissey ferry; www.mevagissey-ferries.co.uk
Of interest	Quiller-Couch memorial, St Wyllow Church, Lanteglos
Facilities	Fowey Car park, Town Quay and Bodinnick Ferry

Directions

One April morning, Fiona, MollieDog and I took the A390 from St Austell, turned right onto the A3082 leading through Par and continued along here following signs to Fowey. We parked in the car park at the top of the town (£4.50 at time of parking for 3-4 hours) and walked down to Town Quay for

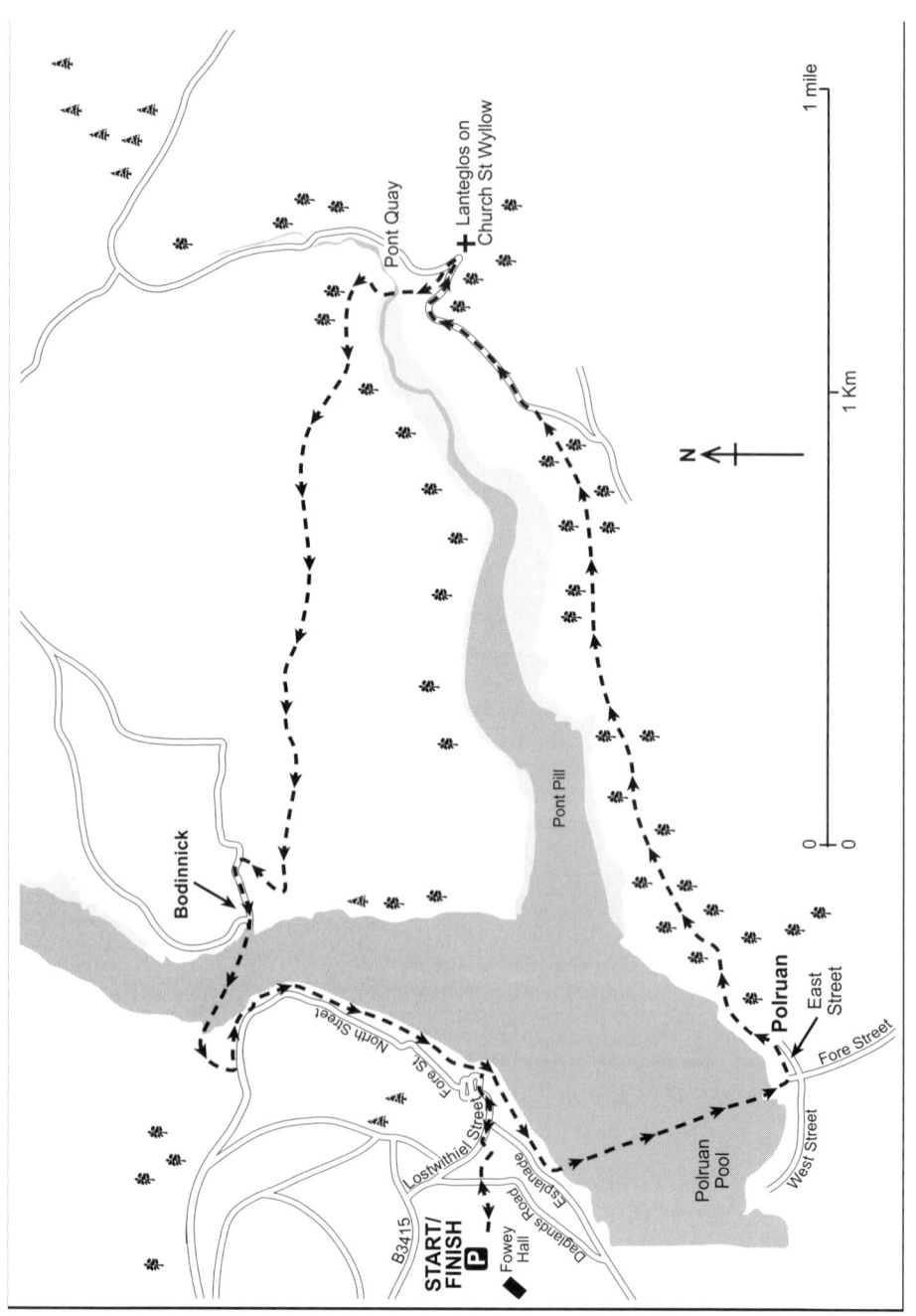

the ferry to Polruan. In summer, the ferry leaves from Whitehouse Slip, along the Esplanade, but there are usually signs in the town indicating where the ferry docks.

Landing at Polruan Quay, we walked past The Lugger and turned right up the hill then followed a sign on the left indicating 'Hall Walk', opposite Crumpet's Tea Shop. The hill is steep here, climbing above Tom's Boatyard, past a variety of well kept cottages. We followed more signs to the Hall Walk, up steep steps and looking over into minute, carefully tended gardens while a tug sounded its horn loudly across the harbour.

Polruan ferry

At the top of these steps is another sign to Hall Walk to the left and we looked over at Fowey, with its shingled roofs glinting in the spring sunshine, while the turrets of Place Manor loomed over the little town. This part of the walk was very muddy and slippery, as we walked past banks of cheerful primroses, stitchwort and violets peeping through. Further along we noted celandines brightening our path, and blackbirds and robins cheeped above us, with the odd startled pheasant squawk, and a coo from a pigeon.

On the left was a sign down into the woods but we ignored this and continued along the main path through the woods past a National Trust sign indicating North Downs. The sunlight slanted through the trees here, illuminating tiny fists of baby ferns unravelling in the spring warmth. This would be a wonderful walk when the bluebells are out – we were a week or two early, but could see their green shoots carpeting the woods.

At a tarmac track, we crossed over to another yellow waymark sign saying Pont and Bodinnick, so we followed that along another path with starry celandines lighting our way, while ivy bloomed from the trees around us. Blackthorn trees blossomed below us, sending gentle white confetti drifting to the ground.

Coming to a fork we turned left, downhill, towards the Fowey River, enjoying the peace: just birds singing and Moll's gentle panting as we strode along. Continuing up the hill we noticed the first campion and goosegrass (which Moll loves) on either side of us, and coming to a sign indicating Pont Pill, we went through a wooden gate, through another muddy section and into a large field, looking back down the valley at spectacular views of the river. At this point, the peace was shattered by what sounded like an argument from Pont Creek below us – presumably a bust up between the seagulls, swans and ducks, but by the time we had got there, they'd sorted out their differences.

Passing through another wooden gate and some steep narrow steps, we could see Pont Creek below us, while Fiona picked wild garlic, just about to come into flower. Along here we came to a sign to Lanteglos Church 340 yards.

St Wyllow was reputedly born in Ireland in 6th century but lived as a hermit in Cornwall until he was beheaded. The current church, dating from the 14th and 15th century and surprisingly large considering its location, contains brasses of the Mohun family from the start of 16th century.

Daphne married Tommy (Boy) Browning at this church in 1932. Wanting a quiet wedding, Daphne arranged it with such speed that the only family members were her parents and cousin. At 7.30am on July 19th 1932, they left Ferryside by boat for Pont bridge and from there walked up to St Wyllow, or Lanteglos church, with Tommy following in his yacht. The early hour was so they could catch the morning tide, and Daphne was delighted to marry in this secret, peaceful church nestled in the countryside. The wedding party adjourned to Ferryside for a wedding breakfast, then Daphne and Tommy changed into sailing gear, jumped back aboard his boat and set off for Frenchman's Creek, where they moored up overnight. Another mysterious, secret location that suited Daphne perfectly.

We followed the path out to a road then through a five barred gate leading up a very steep hill with a stream gurgling beside us as we walked up towards St Wyllow church. When we arrived at the churchyard, it was bathed in sunlight while blackthorn trees waved their delicate confetti above the departed and from inside the church came the sound of a piano playing. Intrigued, we went in to find a young vicar, waiting for the Bishop of St Germans who was apparently walking the Celtic Way, linking various pilgrimage routes from St Germans to St Michael's Mount – a distance of 125 miles. We were told to look out for someone walking with a crook and a purple top, but he must have been delayed for there was no one matching that description on our travels.

Heading back through the hamlet of Whitecross, we retraced our steps to Pont Quay where we had a snack, admiring the restored Pont Pill Farmhouse, which

View along Pont Pill to Polruan

dates from the 18th century, and was The Ship pub at one time. This is a beautiful little sanctuary, much beloved by many writers including Leo Walmsley and Kenneth Grahame, who lived here for a while, though at different times. Pont, or pons, means bridge in Cornish and many years ago this hamlet was an important river quay when sailing barges came upriver to unload coal, fertiliser, limestone, timber, roadstone and fresh produce from the farms in this area of Lanteglos.

Today the scene was tranquil in the spring sunshine: swans swam and sought food in amongst the muddy banks, ducks paddled along the narrow inlet of water, and an egret perched, still as a white statue. Down river, decayed tree roots smothered in black seaweed rose up like silent, prehistoric monsters of the sea. Herons are often seen here, standing sentry on the banks of the river, feeding off frogs, rodents, moles and ducklings.

We crossed the little footbridge, which dates back to 1478, veered to the right and followed the sign to Bodinnick. The path veers sharply to the left, up an uneven slate path, edged with dark violets, shy periwinkles and primroses nestling next door to what turned out to be wild chives. This path continued, in ever increasing steepness, until we reached the top of the hill, where, looking back, we could see Lanteglos church peeping out from the trees and far below us, the tide was edging its way back in, turning the river a milky green.

Coming to a large slate stile, which Moll leapt over like a mountain goat, we arrived in a field and walked along the edge, back along the river. Through another gate, we went over a tiny stream past a National Trust sign indicating Hall Walk, and back through the woods. Here the wild chives grew fatter, amongst the celandines and violets, and Fiona devised impromptu recipes using chives and wild garlic as we walked along.

Emerging from the woods, we blinked in the bright sunshine, absorbing the incredible view in front of us: Polruan's cottages neatly clustered on the side of the hill, like Lego, St Catherine's Castle on the far side of Fowey; a reminder of Fowey's historic past, and a sparkling sea stretching out to Gribben Head's red and white tower in the distance.

Further along, we came to Penleath Point, and the famous monument dedicated to Q, or Sir Arthur Quiller-Couch, who wrote of Fowey, "… the tides of which time has since woven so close into the pulse of my own life that memory cannot now separate the rhythms".

We sat and sunbathed for a while, looking out over a busy Town Quay, Place Manor towering over the houses, and a dinghy with bright red and green sails tacked back and forth in the brisk breeze. In the sleepy distance a cockerel crowed, a seagull wheeled and cried above us and we felt very at peace with the world.

Looking up we noticed a plaque indicating, "The Hall Walk is written of by Carew in his survey of Cornwall published in 1602 as a place of diversified pleasings. It was here, during the Civil War on 17th August 1644 that King Charles narrowly escaped death when a shot killed a poor fisherman who was standing at a place where the King had stood, but a short while before. It is hoped that generations to come will find its prospects pleasing, as did Carew, and will respect its usage accordingly."

Apparently the King was staying with the Mohun family at the time, but Hall Manor was destroyed soon after, during the Civil War. I'm not sure whether Carew intended the poor fisherman's death to be part of the diversified pleasings, but I'm sure Du Maurier wove that into one of her novels somewhere.

Rounding the corner, we walked past a war memorial and noted cherry blossom emerging from an ivy stranglehold – unexpectedly early at the beginning of April. Rejoicing in its ebullient flowers, we were startled by a female pheasant hurtling out of a tree, and took another look back at the perfection of Fowey before descending to the hamlet of Bodinnick, and reaching Ferryside.

The ferry was just coming in as we descended the hill, so we ran on board, past the Old Ferry Inn at Bodinnick, which is well worth a visit, and finally returned to Fowey where we wandered back through town and stopped at the lovely Pinky Murphy's for a coffee and well earned, excellent cake.

From the first time she saw Fowey, Daphne du Maurier had a deep love of the place. She was like a fugitive, arriving at her safe place where she could find peace and solitude, be alone with the sea and nature at its wildest, and write. She could finally be herself.

Even if you aren't a writer, Fowey has a certain magic that might be missing in the crowded summer streets, but on a spring afternoon, with a sparkling sea and a stunning walk where we were so close to nature with every step, I wouldn't have wanted to be anywhere else. I can picture Daphne rising at dawn, taking out her little punt, and rowing her way across the harbour as the sun rose, becoming part of the ancient hills, the rippling river, and the ancient little town. She would explore the very paths that we trod on this walk, along with her dog, Bingo, and later on with her other dogs. Try it and you'll see why it's so magical.

WALK SIX
KILMARTH

The inspiration for *The House on the Strand*

Kilmarth is the ancient dower house of Menabilly, half a mile away, which Daphne moved to after 26 years at Menabilly, shortly after her husband died. Although the lease on Menabilly still had 4 or 5 years to run, Philip Rashleigh wanted her out of Menbilly so that he could move in. After much legal wrangling, during which time Daphne feared she would lose Kilmarth as well as her beloved Menabilly, Rashleigh finally agreed that Daphne could have the lease on Kilmarth for life provided she moved out when the lease expired.

As with Menabilly, she was horrified at the state of Kilmarth and knew she would have to spend a lot of money restoring a house that, yet again, she would never own. Practically it was more suitable for her: it was smaller and lighter, had better views and smaller grounds. But it lacked the mystery and secrecy that bound her to Menabilly. It also meant saying a final goodbye to the memories of when she was young, her time with Tommy, and all the time she had been writing so productively. Having lost Tommy, she was frightened at how leaving Menabilly might affect her.

At the end of June 1969, Daphne finally moved to Kilmarth, having spent the last two years preparing herself and the house and furnishing it with her belongings. The move upset Daphne greatly, and she resented the Rashleighs living in what she felt was her territory – she had made Menabilly her own, and for so many formative, eventful and prolific years. She was also desperately disappointed that her husband, Tommy, died before the move to Kilmarth – he had in fact signed the lease, and she was looking forward to sharing the house with him.

Despite feeling decidedly disorientated, she found Kilmarth a cheerful, welcoming house. But she couldn't bear to see Menabilly, so close, so she kept well away from the grounds. By 1972 she was more settled at Kilmarth and enjoyed having the children to stay as there were separate quarters for the grandchildren. But she had no ideas for another novel, which terrified her. She needed to write.

Then a Mr Thomas of the Old Cornwall Society lent her a full scale tithe map of Tywardreath and she was fascinated to learn that a priory had stood there in the 14th century. Other occupants of the area included a former tenant of Kilmarth, Professor Singer. Some animal embryos were found in bottles in the basement and this gave her the idea of two stories connected by time travelling. These appeared in the collection of short stories entitled, *Not After Midnight* and they were also part of the inspiration for *The House on the Strand*.

Kilmarth is not actually the house on the strand in the book: it is Tiwardrai (which means House on the Strand) which was mentioned in Domesday. Tywardreath is so named because the village was once surrounded by tidal waters on all sides bar the east, and the ground beneath the church was a creek.

Daphne found the science of genetics exciting: she loved the idea that every particle of us has been inherited from our ancestors, so our past is limitless. She felt that scientists were not prepared to acknowledge a sixth sense that can look back into the past or into the future, and she wanted to explore this idea in *The House on the Strand*, combining historical fact with psychological study to produce a novel that was highly unusual and disturbing.

Dick Young accepts his friend Professor Magnus Lane's invitation to stay in his Cornish house for the summer holidays, and act as a guinea pig for his biophysicist friend. Magnus has discovered a new drug that works like a time machine, carrying him back to the 14th century, always to the same setting of the land around Tywardreath. Stepping back in time, like an invisible man, Dick becomes fascinated by the people he sees, and becomes drawn into their lives.

The past becomes much sharper than the present, but if Dick touches anyone or anything, he experiences injury and great pain, hurtles abruptly back to the present, and suffers extreme nausea, vertigo and shakes as well as a bloodshot eye.

Magnus also has concerns about the physical dangers of the drug: while under the influence, Dick could well be run over, or badly hurt, because parts of the brain shut down. Like driving when drunk, the functional part of the brain still controls movements, but the danger is always there, and it seems that there is no warning from one part of the brain to another.

Magnus suggests that when taking the drug, part of the brain is susceptible to reversal, going back to an earlier time in its chemical history. But why does he always go back to that specific time? Every time Dick travels back, Roger the horseman is there to act as interpreter: although the people speak Mediaeval French, Dick can understand them perfectly.

Retreating into the past, he becomes increasingly involved and troubled by the people he meets and ignores any thoughts of his own future, to the distress of his wife and family. He feels very much that he belongs among the people he meets; that he is one of them, even if they don't know he is there. He is at once living in his own time as well as theirs. But as the story continues, Dick starts to become confused between the past and the present: his two worlds begin to merge and he loses track of what is happening in each one.

Dick is convinced that he and Roger are each other's keepers, and all the characters are bound together, through time forever, so death has no meaning. In becoming the various characters in the past, he somehow becomes more himself – which is presumably what Daphne felt, as she was writing. In Dick's case, this hallucination is a way of escaping his own life – the lives of those he meets in the 14th century seem infinitely more fascinating than his own. And the more time he spends with them, the deeper he becomes involved, pulled by his alter ego, Roger, until his sanity becomes at risk. By the end of the book, Dick discovers that the drug is a very powerful hallucinogen that is so toxic it can seriously affect the central nervous system, which can lead to paralysis.

Daphne got so involved writing it, that she felt she'd become Dick and couldn't bear to leave the novel for more than a few hours. She said she woke up feeling sick and dizzy one day, as Dick does, from taking the drug. So, walking with Dick, she too became involved in the past – as she had when writing about the Jane Slade, and those who had lived and died at Menabilly. She lived through their stories and their emotions, but felt their vulnerability as she knew they had already died.

The House on the Strand was Daphne du Maurier's favourite book, which she wrote almost as a film script, hoping it would be made into a film. She was disappointed that it never was.

What you need to know	
Distance	4 miles
Allow	2½ hours
Suggested Map	OS Explorer 107 St Austell & Liskeard
Starting point	Tywardreath church; grid reference SX 085543
Terrain	Moderate, few steep hills
Nearest refreshments	New Inn, Tywardreath www.staustellbrewery.co.uk/pub/tywardreath/new-inn
Public transport	Buses 24, 214, 293 & 296 Par railway station 5 minute walk
Of interest	Site of Priory. Fowey Festival May each year
Facilities	None

Directions

One Saturday in early April, Deb, Rich, MollieDog and I headed for St Austell, took the A390 and turned off to Par, then continued on the A3082. From Tehidy Road we turned into Well Street in Tywardreath, and parked in Priory Lane, near the church, where a cherry blossom flowered exuberantly.

The Benedectine Priory featured in *The House on the Strand*, which would have been on the land at the bottom of Priory Hill, was founded in approximately 1135, and was the sister Priory to St Sergius and Bacchus of Angers, in Brittany. After the dissolution of the monasteries in 1536, the Priory was vandalised to the point of destruction. Some of the stone was to be taken back to Angers by sea, but the ship sank at the entrance to Fowey harbour and some of the stone was recovered in the last century and taken to Menabilly. (Presumably the rest reappeared in local farms and houses nearby.) The only remains of the Priory are over the door of a house in Church Street, where there is a carving of the Virgin and Child. The Priory possessions included the church, St Sampson's Chapel at Golant and huge nearby estates. The monks were a corrupt, drunken and dissolute bunch, as described in *The House on the Strand*, and knowing it was true adds to the fascinating reading.

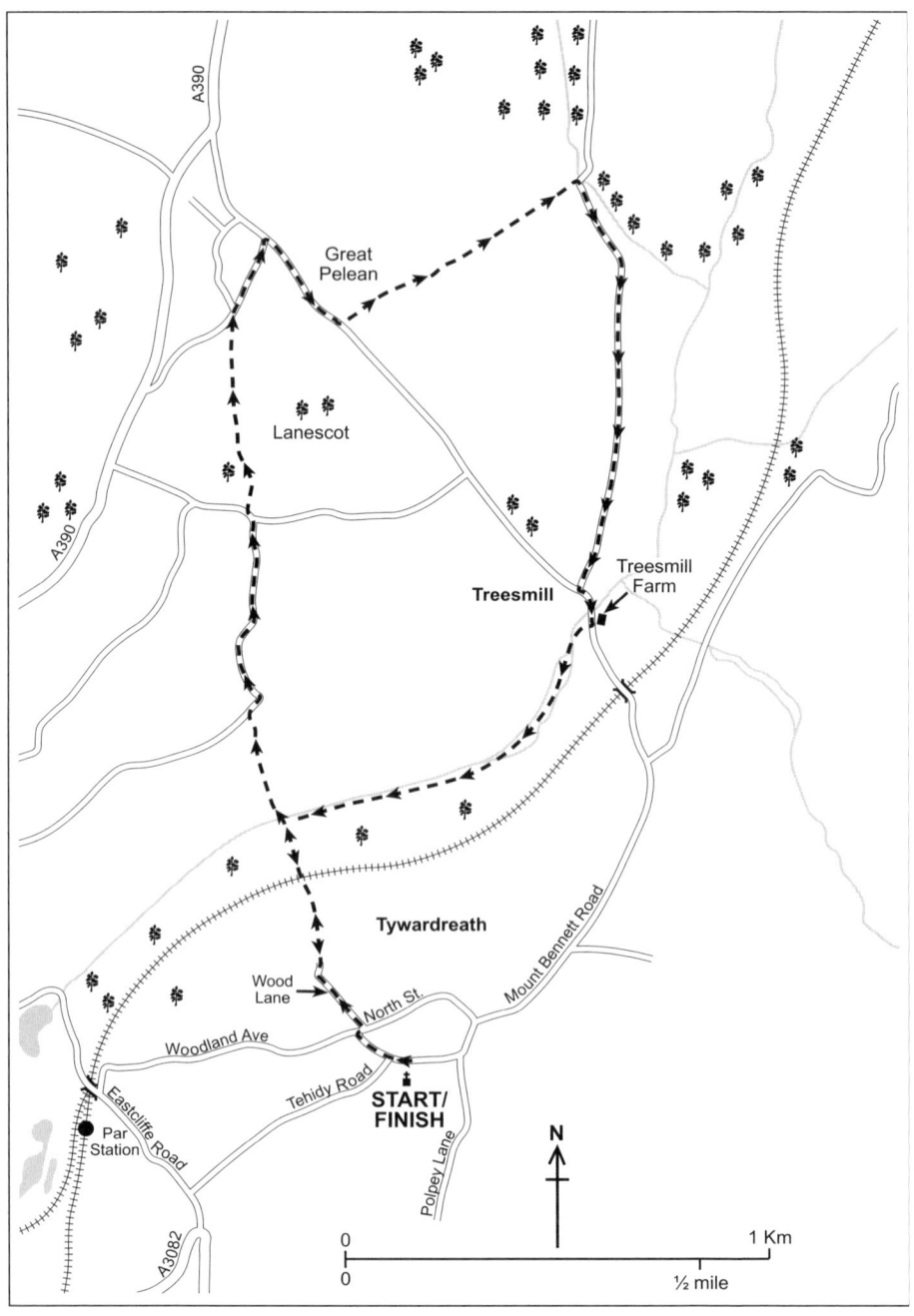

Today, we walked along Church Street in the sunshine past a 'Saints Way' sign indicating St Blazey Bridge 2m and turned into Woodland Avenue, and continued into Wood Lane, past another Saints' Way sign then turned right and almost immediately left, onto a public footpath and a further Saints' Way sign.

Walking down a steep and rocky path edged with pillows of celandine and wild garlic, birds tweeted noisily overhead while we inhaled the heady scent of the garlic. Carefully stepping over a huge, bewildered bumble bee, we found the path levelled out and we passed underneath a railway bridge that made me think of Magnus and Dick's wanderings around this area – in Magnus's case, with fatal consequences. What would they have seen and how has the land changed since Du Maurier wrote *The House on the Strand*?

Celtic cross at Tywardreath churchyard

The railway bridge led to a flat path where we crossed a footbridge and came to a mini-canal known locally as Crocodile Swamp. We followed the path over the second footbridge and up a steep and stony path lit by celandines. At the top of this hill we turned right and followed a quiet road to Lanescot, past blue periwinkles and primroses nestling in the hedges. It was hot out of the wind, and the only sound was of birds loudly tweeting the arrival of spring, and the steady rumble of farm machinery in the distance.

Passing East Lanescot Farm, we came to a junction overlooking the Luxulyan Valley, crossed the road and continued up a track by Berry Brow house. We turned right along a public footpath sign, climbing uphill all the while, with stunning views over the patchwork of fields, and the wooded areas of

Bridge at Crocodile Swamp

Luxulyan. We passed an allotment on our right, admired the gorse in flower and a friendly bay horse came up in search of food – Deb picked the grass on our side of the fence which looked tastier for him. In another field were shaggy goats with impressively curled horns, while alongside them grazed delicate, snow white goats with chocolate brown faces.

"I can see the sea!" cried Rich, the first to reach the top of the hill, as we joined him and rejoiced in the shimmering sheets of water in the distance, almost indistinguishable against the sky. Had Dick climbed this very path, I wondered, and looked out as we did now? If so, was he in the 14th century or his own? And did he have time to appreciate the wonders of the spring sunshine?

The banks were ablaze with celandines, stitchwort and campion as we followed a dusty path round and looked out over a tree lined valley beyond St Blazey, while two very beautiful black geldings trotted up to us, their coats gleaming in the sunshine. At the end of this footpath we turned right into a road and climbed uphill past a rhododendron bush with scarlet flouncy flowers like a flamenco dancer's skirt.

We turned right at the top of this hill, past Carrigatt Farm and headed downhill, while horses neighed in the distance and a crow croaked overhead.

Around us was a tapestry of fields and trees, horses, farms, and further on, a mine shaft on our right, from which ivy sprouted like a wayward haircut. Coming to Great Pelean Farm we turned left; although there is no public footpath sign here, it is marked as a footpath on the OS map. We walked through the farmyard surrounded by farming machinery and cattle on our right, with chickens clucking on our left, until we came to a narrow muddy path with a trickle of a stream running down the middle.

Heading down the path, with high hedges on either side, I laughed at Moll's drooling focus on Rich who was eating a Scotch egg (she is incredibly greedy). Primroses dotted the banks on either side as we walked along, with endless fields of varying colours on either side. There was little sign of habitation here: you could almost smell how old the land is, and we could have been back in the 14th century had it not been for the whine of a distant chainsaw.

At the end of the lane we turned right along a quiet road and, further on, a restored copper mine (now an impressive looking house). Tales of the past almost ooze from the ground: no wonder Du Maurier wrote such a powerful novel here. Tales of the past almost ooze from the ground. I wondered if the monks had wandered this far in search of food, or if Roger Kylmerth had relatives who lived along here. A tractor ploughed in the field on our right, turning the earth over into rich clods of earth like chocolate fudge.

Coming to another road, we turned left into Treesmill, past Bridgefield farm and a stall selling marmalade and kindling. Walking over the picturesque bridge over a stream, we turned right at the public footpath sign and followed the path along by the river Fowey, which turned into the mini-canal we'd crossed earlier in the walk. Here we met a gathering of Rich's fellow geocachers, who exchanged views of the local geocaches before going in opposite directions. Geocaching is an outdoor treasure hunt, whereby a container holding an item or several items is hidden at a particular location for GPS users to find by means of coordinates posted on the Internet. It's growing in popularity with people of all ages, and Rich loves it.

Along by the river, this was the perfect spring walk, ablaze with celandines, and every tree's leaves bursting forth. The water sparkled with unseen gems, and we marvelled at its clarity, at the little fish darting over the pebbly bottom. Coming to the footbridge, we returned the way we came, along the path, under the railway bridge and up the steep path and back to Tywardreath, where we adjourned to the New Inn and met Mike, alias

Pencoise, another geocache friend who was a mine of information concerning the area.

He told us that the land around here used to be tidal all the way to Treesmill, and the marshland was drained which was how Par came into existence: barges would come up to the priory at Tywardreath. He also said that the people of Tywardreath have formed a group to start proceedings for a dig to find the Priory, and are applying for grant and lottery funding schemes to help fund the project.

Daphne was a great researcher, and loved the history of Cornwall, so I would like to think she would approve of this scheme. But looking down into the marshy valley, we could see where much of the novel takes place, could almost see the beautiful Isolde Carminowe, watch Roger go about his duties, hear the monks squabbling and the clip clop of horses' hooves. It left us with a real sense of time long ago that Daphne du Maurier evokes so well.

WALK SEVEN
GRIBBIN HEAD

Daphne's regular stamping ground from Menabilly

When the Du Maurier family bought Ferryside, they became interested in the important local families, including the Rashleighs, whose principal house was Menabilly. It was originally built in 1624 in a hidden valley, to keep it safe from enemies – which made it all the more difficult to find. But Daphne, intrigued by hearing that the house was severely neglected, finally succeeded in locating it after several failed attempts.

Most of the events that took place in Daphne du Maurier's novels took place near the houses of Menabilly, and, later, Kilmarth. This was her stamping ground, where she walked her two white West Highland terriers, several times a day, over the fields, down to Polridmouth Bay and up to Gribben Head.

So what was it about this house that drew Du Maurier so? Her relationship with Menabilly was the driving force in her life for many years – but rather like a mistress, loving a man she cannot marry, Daphne was never able to buy Menabilly. She rented it, poured money, love and adoration into it, and lived in it for 26 years. But it was never truly hers. She always lived with the threat of having to leave it, and return it to its owners.

In her short story, *The House of Secrets*, Du Maurier describes how she first tried to find Menabilly . She and her sister, Angela, found the lodge at Four Turnings, opened the creaking iron gates and crept down the drive while around them the trees on either side loomed, darker and more menacing as dusk arrived. They were driven back by lack of daylight, but she knew she would return, and one morning got up at sunrise, rowed across the harbour to Pridmouth, where she left her boat and climbed up a narrow path leading to the woods.

She arrived at sunrise this time, to find a house with shuttered windows, and such an air of mystery surrounding it that Daphne felt the house was fast asleep, never to be woken. Looking at it, she fell in love, and from that moment on, it was as if the house owned her. She longed to bring it to life, feeling that in doing so, she could bring a dormant part of herself alive.

But it took seventeen years before an opportunity arose to live there. Daphne was living in Sussex while the war was on, when she heard that there was to be a sale at Menabilly. Dr Rashleigh had decided to sell the contents and let it for a peppercorn rent until he died and his cousin inherited the estate. Arriving back in Cornwall, she crept back to see the house, which had deteriorated badly. She was determined to save it, and approached her lawyer who, to everyone's amazement, eventually returned with news that she could rent the house. But it would be impossible to live there, given the state of it.

There was also a catch: the 20 year lease dictated that the house should be maintained at the cost of the tenant. A new roof was needed immediately, as well as many other major repairs. Everyone thought she was mad, but Daphne was determined to have the house, and in August 1943 she signed the lease. By Christmas that year she had transformed the house and the family had moved in. The ivy had all gone, the windows had new frames, and all the

What you need to know	
Distance	4 miles approximately
Allow	2 hours
Suggested Map	OS Explorer 107 St Austell & Liskeard
Starting point	Coombe Farm car park; grid reference: SX 110512
Terrain	Few steep hills
Nearest refreshments	Coombe Farm cream teas and B&B: www.coombefarmbb.co.uk 01726 833616
Public transport	Nearest rail station is Par; Buses: 24/25
Of interest	Gribben Head, owned by National Trust, open to the public on occasions
Facilities	No public toilets on this route

rooms had been redecorated. There was a new roof, new plumbing, and despite the heating being inadequate for the large rooms and freezing corridors, Daphne was delighted. Menabilly was her haven, where she could write, she could keep her family safe, and keep unwanted visitors away.

In *Daphne du Maurier's Cornwall*, she wrote, "At midnight, when the children were asleep and all was hushed and still, the house would whisper her secrets, and the secrets would turn to stories. In those days, in some eerie fashion, we became one, the house and I".

Directions

From St Austell, Mel, MollieDog and I took the A390 towards Fowey and turned onto the A3082 through St Blazey and Par. At Four Turnings roundabout, we took the exit signed to Fowey Town Centre and just after that is a small lane on the right called Prickly Post Lane. This led to Lankelly Lane; we turned right and continued until we reached the National Trust car park at Coombe Farm and parked there.

From here we walked towards the far end of the car park, through a little wooden gate and turned left into a grassy lane with high hedges on either side. It was a beautiful late summer's day when we did this walk, with a languid sun beating down from a cloudless sky, and a lazy bumble bee buzzing above our heads. Pink campion peeked from bunches of nettles, overlaid with bracken in both hedges, still green on this October afternoon.

At the end of the lane, we went through another gate and skirted a field with Menabilly Woods down below us, and the Gribbin daymark a distant red and white blob at the

Red and white Gribben tower

top of the hill, in front of us. Passing a five barred wooden gate, we skirted the left hand boundary of the field which led us to a kissing gate and a steep lane leading down to Polridmouth Beach (pronounced Pridmouth).

This lane was rocky underfoot, but shady due to the sycamore and beech trees on either side of us, and from here we could see the cottage and ornamental lake fed by a stream far up in the Menabilly estate. The lake dates from between the First and Second World War and was used as a decoy for Fowey Harbour. At least one bomb was diverted from Fowey, and it was estimated that around 5% of German bombs were diverted by decoys, saving thousands of lives across the whole of Britain.

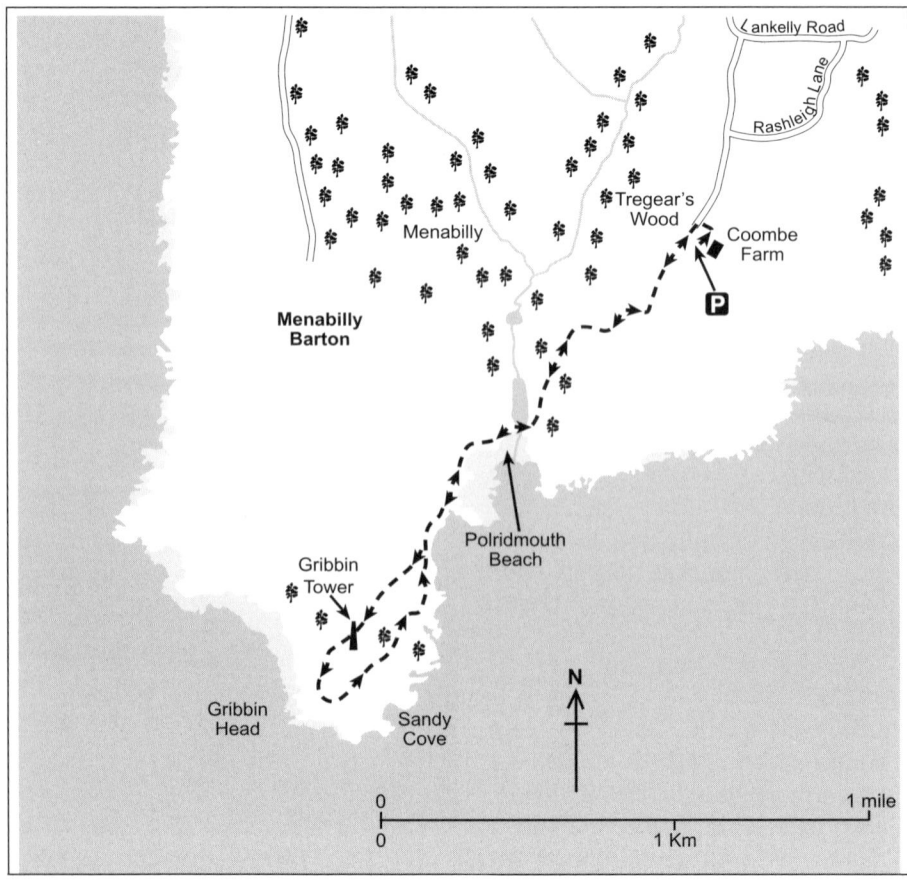

Poldridmouth Bay

In January 1930, the *Romanie*, a three masted 100 ft iron sailing ship, was returning to Par from Fowey when she was caught in a storm, lost power and drifted onto the rocks in Polridmouth Bay. Her captain and crew managed to escape, but the ship was wrecked. When Daphne Du Maurier walked along this beach, it was the wreck of the *Romanie* that inspired her to make the beach the setting for the murder of her character, Rebecca, and the wreck of her boat.

Sadly there is no public access to Menabilly, and because of the woodland, very little of the house can be seen from any public road or footpath. But it was good to know that it was there, hidden among the trees. Descending to the beach, we joined others paddling in rock pools, having picnics and enjoying the sunshine – some swimming and several people standing on the edge of the sand, mystifyingly carrying a fishing rod that dangled out over the sand. Perhaps no one had told them that they needed water to catch fish?

We followed the coastal footpath away from Polridmouth round to the next cove where a barbecue was lit – always an occupational hazard with MollieDog around, as she wishes to partake uninvited. Thankfully they weren't actually cooking, so we continued unscathed.

The Gribbin was originally one of the warning beacons at the time of the Armada, and at the end of the 18th century was one of several naval signal

Path leading to Poldridmouth Beech, Gribben in the distance

stations for defence against a possible French invasion: the ruins can still be seen near the daymark. Gribbin, or Gribben, comes from the Cornish meaning the crest of a bird, or a little ridge.

The daymark is an 84 foot red and white striped 84 foot tower, built in 1832 by Trinity House to prevent sailors from mistaking the Gribbin for St Anthony Head, and sailing into the shallow waters of St Austell Bay rather than the deep waters of Falmouth Harbour. William Rashleigh of Menabilly offered the land and stone from a quarry on the headland and asked that, in return, the tower would be 'an ornament to my grounds'.

Past Polridmouth, we continued along boardwalks shrouded with bamboos. Further on, the path twists up through the trees with the last blackberries peeking forth – it's said that the devil spits on them after October 1st, but in that case my guts must be devil proof, for they tasted sweeter than ever. We could see rock pools glinting down on the beach, and further on we came to a waymark sign pointing up towards Gribbin with a bright emerald green field on our right as we walked along tracks of clover.

The path descended to another little cove, and looking back towards Fowey we could see several yachts enjoying the fine weather and fresh wind, and, far out on an indigo sea, three fishing boats, gulls trailing in their wake. After a sign asking us to keep dogs under control, we passed through a last gate and started the steep pull up towards Gribbin. It was easy to see why Daphne and her husband Tommy would do this walk most days – it affords the most spectacular views back 30 miles to Rame Head near Plymouth, and in the other direction to Dodman: on a day like this, we couldn't imagine wanting to be anywhere else.

The Rashleighs planted the woods here to enhance their view of the house (Menabilly), and in spring the woods are filled with bluebells, campion, primroses, garlic and other joys.

The last climb up to the Gribbin was steep – even Moll was panting – and, pausing for a pitstop half way up the hill, we enjoyed the long autumn shadows stretching across the fields, the shimmering sea that turned turquoise, dark blue and green in places, making us think we were in the Mediterranean, not Cornwall. Passing sycamore and hawthorn trees, we finally made it to the top, where we explored the tower and views out over St Austell Bay, the long stretch of sand that is Carlyon Bay and the far headland of Black Head.

From here we were intending to walk to Polkerris, over to Tregaminion and back to Lankelly Farm, but we were running out of time, so we decided to return via the coastal footpath round Gribben Head. Leaves rustled and whispered in the trees as we walked, and there was a slight chill in the air which made walking all the more pleasant. Looking down, the cliffs were incredibly steep along this stretch of the coast, but I kept my mind off vertigo as we passed the bright red berries of Old Man's Beard.

We came across a fine selection of fungus along here, including one like a huge white plate, but as Mel had left her Collins book of mushrooms at home, we decided not to pick any but took photos and admired them from a safe distance.

Passing through a gate, we walked through rowan trees. The bracken had started to turn brown along here, giving forth a sweet nutty smell, and as we walked we became aware of what sounded like a church bell, ringing from under the waves. This is the Cannis Rock south cardinal marker – a bell buoy that guards the dangerous Cannis Rock that dries out at 4.3 metres. There are many bell buoys around the coast which are spooky at night or in fog but a brilliant, very old invention.

View from Gribben

We passed hawthorn and gorse bushes – with amazingly, no gorse blooms – and all the trees leaning inwards, brushed by the prevailing south westerly winds into a lopsided hairstyle. Following this twisty path, we enjoyed the crunch of the first autumn leaves under our feet, while the bell buoy tolled in the distance, like some ghost church, interspersed with the roar of the waves below. The languid light of autumn caught the tree trunks, wound round with throttling ivy, while shafts of sunlight illuminated the golden bracken and ochre fern fronds.

Here we passed a wonderful selection of ferns of all shapes and sizes, rhododendrons and beech trees, before we emerged out of this wooded area of Gribben Head, into the sunlit afternoon – like coming out of the cinema in daylight, we blinked at the sudden brilliance.

For the first time this year, we could feel autumn in the cool of the shade, so we relished the warmth of the sun as we headed downhill, past a fat little robin sitting in the path ahead of us. When we reached Polridmouth on the way back, we sat on the rocks and sunbathed, watching a father and child splashing and giggling in the sea, while a young dog sat on the beach, eyeing them anxiously.

There is a famous picture of Daphne walking through the fields from Polridmouth with her three children: she must often have sat on this beach, watching her children swim, while the dogs ran up and down the beach.

We were enjoying the late afternoon sun so much that we nearly got cut off by the tide, and had to scramble over the rocks to join the path back up the hill. We walked up the path, past a windblown oak tree, with leaves delicately fluttering in the breeze like shaky fingers waving to us. A late bee buzzed lazily, settling on the last of the honeysuckle, before drifting away out of sight.

Everything looked at its best on this October afternoon, from the rosehips peeking out of the hedges, to the clouds building on the horizon. This was a perfect way to welcome in autumn, and a perfect tribute to the great writer herself. We really were walking in her footsteps.

WALK EIGHT
CASTLE-AN-DINAS

Location for the dramatic ending of *Castle Dor*

Castle-an-Dinas is one of the biggest, impressive hill forts in Cornwall, built on the top of Castle Downs, with wonderful panoramic views of both north and south coasts and across central Cornwall. Castle-an-Dinas was one of the Duke of Cornwall's seats and according to legend, both Cador, the Duke of Cornwall, and Ygraine, King Arthur's mother were killed here. It is reputed to be the hunting lodge of King Arthur, and near St Columb there used to be a stone, now lost, which was supposed to bear the four hoofprints his horse made while out hunting.

Castle Dor was a novel started by Sir Arthur Quiller-Couch, known as Q, who died in 1944 leaving it unfinished. In 1959, his daughter, Foy, who was a close friend of Daphne, asked if she would finish the novel: Daphne felt honoured to be asked, but was nervous in case she couldn't live up to expectations. Chapter Seventeen is thought to be where du Maurier takes over the novel, but she has matched her style of writing so closely to Q's that it is impossible to mark the exact takeover. She added some extra dialogue and the novel was finally published in 1962 under both their names with a preface by Foy Quiller-Couch.

Daphne first met Q when she was living at Ferryside. Q was also a resident of Fowey, in a house along the Esplanade called The Haven, and he became a valued mentor and friend to the budding writer. She also became friends with Foy, and it was while they were out riding on Bodmin Moor one day, and got lost, that she conceived the idea of *Jamaica Inn*.

Q was rowing up the river towards Lantyan with Foy when he saw 'Mark's Gate' on a map, and from then on he was hooked on the Tristan and Iseult story. *Castle Dor* is set mostly around the Fowey river in the mid 19th century when Amyot Trestane, a young Breton sailor, falls in love with Linnet Lewarne, recently married to a much older man. Their love affair re-enacts that of Tristan and Iseult: Linnet becomes Iseult, Amyot Tristan, and Linnet's husband Mark Lewarne becomes Iseult's husband, King Mark. Q introduced a character named Doctor Carfax as the commentator, who controls the events of the novel.

Daphne and her husband, Tommy, retraced the events of Tristan and Iseult, and she familiarised herself with the local landscape including Castle Dor, the Iron Age Hill fort near Fowey, and Castle-an-Dinas near Indian Queens, where the climax of the novel takes place. Running through the novel is the theme of re-enactment; the present day characters are powerless over their destiny as they are merely replaying events that happened thousands of years before: there is no way of changing the inevitable outcome.

Towards the end of the novel, Mr Tregentil, a patient of Dr Carfax, has been researching the Tristan legend and believes that his family may have lived at Castle-an-Dinas many years ago. He declares an interest in visiting the fort – "the greatest earthwork in the whole of Cornwall". The Bosanko children, whom Amyot looks after, are longing to go too, so it is decided he will accompany them.

It is arranged that the party will stay at Tresaddern Farm, for Dr Carfax's housekeeper's sister lives there and takes in visitors. Linnet knows that her husband has a landlords' dinner at the Indian Queen inn, not far from Castle-an-Dinas, and she and Amyot arrange to meet secretly at the Castle early one afternoon.

When Amyot, the children and Mr Tregentil arrive at Castle-an-Dinas, Amyot has a strong sense that he has been here before, and guides them to the entrance of the hill fort without consulting a map. Without being told, he knows where to find fresh spring water, and directs the party to the centre of the castle, where he knows it will be drier, overlooking the northern rampart, leaving the others puzzled as to how he knows so much about the place. But Amyot is troubled by the place, perhaps sensing his end: "All my friends… bearing me here to die".

The plans go awry. First, the weather is against them: Mark and his wife hit thick fog and don't arrive at the Indian Queen inn until after 2 pm, whereas Linnet and Amyot had arranged to meet between 1 and 2. Linnet is beside

Tresaddern Farm

herself, but accepts a tumbler of cider, intending to hurry to her rendezvous with Amyot, little realising that her husband has slipped a draught into her drink, and quickly she falls asleep.

Meanwhile, realising that Linnet must have become lost in the fog, Amyot walks to the Indian Queen inn and blags his way in, pretending to be a musician, offering entertainment for the landlords' dinner.

When Dr Carfax belatedly hears about the planned trip, he hastens to try and stop the lovers meeting, and encounters Mr Tregentil. They discuss the two possible versions of the Tristan legend: it appears that current events are following the second, less popular version, where the maid betrays her mistress to King Mark. When he finds Tristan singing to Iseult, he wounds him with a poisoned spear and locks Iseult in her room to stop her following Tristan. He runs to his friend, Dinas, but dies at the castle, and the Queen gets there too late to say goodbye.

At this point in the discussion, Dr Carfax's horse goes lame due to a stone in his hoof, which Dr Carfax removes with his pocket knife before finally arriving at the Indian Queen inn, where he discovers Lewarne and Amyot fighting. Amyot leaps out of the window and runs off, and Dr Carfax discovers that Linnet has been drugged by her husband to prevent her running off.

Unsure what has happened to Linnet, he tells Mark that his wife must be taken to the nearest hospital, in Bodmin, as soon as possible, and Dr Carfax returns to the mine at the foot of Castle-an-Dinas, where he guesses Amyot has gone, as Tristan did, thousands of years back. Sure enough, he finds Amyot, convinced he is Tristan: but he has fallen into a pit and his foot is caught in wire.

Trapped in the past, Amyot is convinced that Dr Carfax has come to harm him, and wrestles with him, seizing the knife from the doctor's pocket and threatening to cut his throat. The doctor wrenches his wrist aside, and in so doing drives the knife into Amyot's shoulder. He staunches the wound and cleans it hurriedly, for now there are two patients to go to hospital, both in danger of losing their lives. Too late, Dr Carfax realises grimly that his knife, full of grime and grit from removing the horse's hoof stone, has played the role of the poisoned spear.

While this is going on, Linnet calls to Amyot from her sleep, but Amyot, returning to the present, is told that she is nowhere near and, losing all hope of ever seeing her again, he dies, while Linnet fades away in her sleep.

What you need to know	
Distance	3½ miles
Allow	1¾ hours
Suggested Map	OS Explorer 106 Newquay and Padstow
Starting point	Car park at Castle-an-Dinas; grid reference SW 946620
Terrain	Moderate
Nearest refreshments	None
Public transport	None at time of walking
Of interest	Castle-an-Dinas hill fort
Facilities	None

Directions

On that cheerful note, one sunny morning in late May, Mr B, MollieDog and I set off to find Castle-an-Dinas. We both had separate ideas of how to get there,

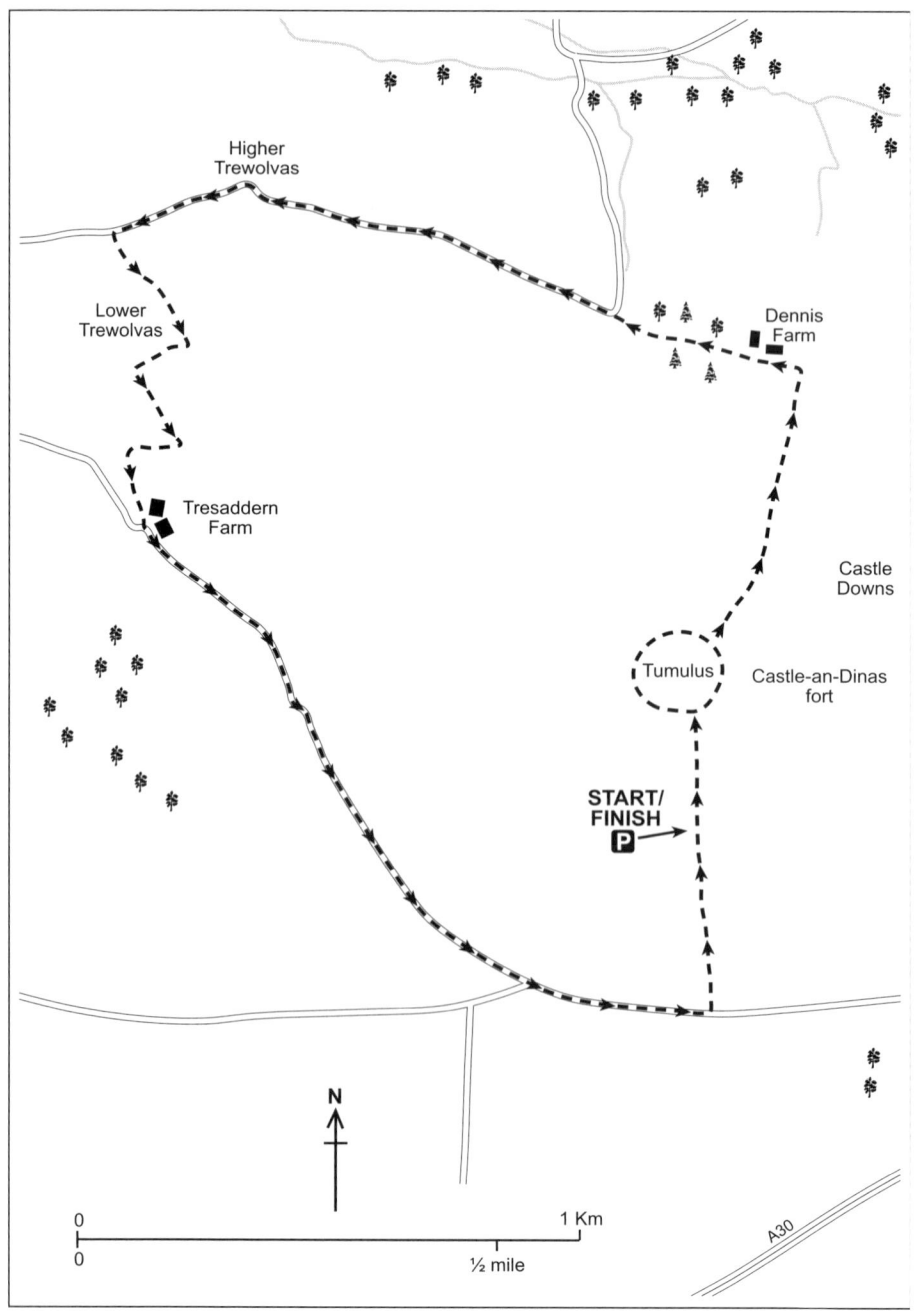

despite having looked at the map, and unfortunately I was eating a cheese roll when he said, "So we don't need to turn off here then?" as we sailed past the turning to Indian Queens. I shan't repeat the ensuing conversation, except to say that I abandoned my roll and it took another hour before we finally arrived at our destination.

However, any sensible travellers will take the A30 and turn off at the Indian Queens junction. From here head north to St Francis Road and continue to Moorland Road. After five minutes, turn right and continue to Castle-an-Dinas, where you will see a brown historic monument sign. Turn up the gravelled drive until you come to a large parking area (marked on the OS map) and start the walk here.

We headed through a kissing gate leading up onto Castle Downs and headed uphill to reach the fort ramparts, while skylarks swooped and soared around us, trying to deflect Moll from their nests. Reaching the ramparts, we walked around the hill fort which is 700m above sea level, and has a diameter of 85 metres.

From the sheer size and positioning of this fort, it's clear that this would have been the base for the kings that ruled Cornwall before the Norman Conquest – the other hill forts around the county were merely watch towers and outposts of minor rulers. Du Maurier and her husband did a lot of research about the area, and Tommy, with his soldier's knowledge, told her that Castle-an-Dinas was so high and in such an excellent position that the inhabitants could have defended themselves against any invaders. There was plenty of space here to accommodate sleeping quarters and dining areas for an army of warriors, as well as plenty of stabling, granaries and bakehouses.

The fort is surrounded by three ramparts and ditches, one of which is markedly smaller, indicating that it may have been occupied earlier. There is also speculation that there were several entrances and so this is the remains of a Neolithic causewayed enclosure which would mean its origins were even earlier.

Walking along a path we could see both north and south coasts and in the centre of the fort, we came to an information plinth which told us what could be seen from this point, on a clear day: Brown Willy in the far distance, and Newquay, Watergate Bay and Mawgan Porth off to the west.

View from Castle-an-Dinas

Taking time to admire these incredibly impressive views, we then turned right, going east, and followed a path round the bank till we came to a gap in the ramparts by a hawthorn tree and walked through here, past the first foxgloves, through the outer ramparts, and took a path to the left, to a wooden kissing gate. This path led downhill to another wooden kissing gate and in between two wire fences.

At our feet we came across a wonderfully furry caterpillar: an elephant hawk apparently, and Mr B warned about this being viper country. As adder bites are very dangerous to dogs, often proving fatal if not treated within minutes, Mr B led the way as we walked downhill with a pleasant breeze blowing. On our left, the scrubby area used to be Cornwall's largest tungsten mine from 1916 to 1957, though it was closed in 1950 as, after the Second World War, tungsten could be imported cheaply from the USA. As a result, the area is dotted with open mine shafts so please keep to the paths. Ore was taken from the mine down the hill to be processed near Denis Farm.

Heading downhill towards the woods, on either side of us, grassy fields were studded with buttercups, daisies and campion, dotted with the last of the bluebells – nature is so clever at arranging her spring/summer wardrobe. Coming to a wooden kissing gate, we passed a derelict building and followed a path into the woods, with ivy wound round many of the beech trunks, and ferns of the palest green emerging. Walking on a carpet of fallen pine needles and baby fir cones, we followed the path out of the woods and onto a track where we turned left.

Denis Farm lay before us on the right, with abandoned old tractor parts, a motorbike tank and many other gems that had Mr B enthralled. Passing a campervan, we saw a couple of butterflies dancing together in the sunshine – an act of courtship maybe – as we continued down a beech tree lined path with rhododendrons on our left and saffron yellow fields of buttercups on our right. This is also a popular spot for woodpeckers: although we heard some, we weren't lucky enough to see any, though we saw the telltale round holes in several trunks which indicate they had nested.

Going through another farm gate we continued along a metalled track which curved round to a dusty lane with a murder of crows in the fields on our right. Ahead of us was Trevithick East Farm, and a church on the left, as we enjoyed hedges of campion, alexander and the very last of the bluebells, a little faded by now. Tangled, gnarled roots of sycamore trees twined round the hedges and a black and white calf staggered on wobbly legs to say hello to us.

At Lower Trewarvas Farm, we saw a collection of very old scythes in a barn and past that, a farmer sharpening a chainsaw while a collie looked on, barking at us intruders. Just past the farm, opposite a Dutch barn, is a layby on the left and an overgrown footpath which leads uphill. There is no sign to this path and it's easy to overlook it (we did at first) but we walked along, trying to dodge the nettles – not easy as I was wearing shorts – and new ferns of the palest green.

Halfway up we came to a gate with a yellow waymark sign pointing ahead, and past a big holly bush, we continued past an old water pumping system covered in ivy and honeysuckle. This is a long, gentle slope leading upwards and presumably not many people venture along here, for it was very overgrown. Squeezing underneath a fallen tree, we inhaled the earthy, rich smell of wild garlic, thinking this would be an even better walk when the bluebells are first out, and wondered what the track was used for originally – as a route between farms perhaps?

Coming to a gate into a field with horse jumping fences, we turned right by some solar panels and skirted the field, past sycamore and ash trees, with blackbirds singing loudly and clearly above us. This path leads round to the left and to another gate which led into Tresaddern Farm, with several staddle stones on the lawn and a duck pond in the distance. Staddle, or mushroom stones, are usually around 100 years old, and were traditionally used as bases to support hayricks, lifting them off the ground so that rats and other vermin couldn't climb up and eat the hay. The supporting stone also enabled air to circulate round the hay or grain, so keeping it dry.

Tresaddern is where Amyot, Mr Tregentil and the Bosanko children, Mary and Johnny, stayed in preparation for their trip to Castle-an-Dinas. It is described as: "... the farmhouse itself a manor in days gone by, rugged, strong, with space enough once for seigneur and his family and a pack of servants besides. Mona's sister had done well for herself, with this snug holding, deep enough in the sheltered valley to withstand wind and weather".

Moll and the staddle stones

Nowadays the farm and buildings have been refurbished to provide a tranquil, secluded setting (apart from the geese). Ducks waddled and quacked among the grass, and the surrounding buildings were quiet, maybe unoccupied, but gave the impression they were simply watching, waiting. Maybe for us to get lost...

The route we had planned to take didn't exist, so we had to backtrack and continue past Tresaddern farmhouse on the left, where we were approached by a couple of geese, protesting at our presence. We hurried up the road, evading the raucous geese, noticing, strangely, scallop shells in the hedgerows and what seemed like a magpie's nest in some branches above us. Foxgloves towered out of the hedges as the clouds gathered and the temperature dropped rapidly.

Coming to a give way sign, we found ourselves at the main road, turned left and walked a short way along before coming to the sign to Castle-an-Dinas where we turned left, walked up the flinty drive and found ourselves back at the car park.

Looking back over the moors, the fog had come down in a dense duvet, obscuring the Cornish Alps – the spoils from the china clay pits near St Austell which formed huge white mountainous peaks.

The house behind us had also been swallowed up, along with the remains of the Castle: everything was blotted out, leaving no sense of where we were, or what era – just as it did so many years ago when Linnet and Mark were trying to get to the Indian Queens Inn for their final fateful meeting….

WALK NINE
PENDENNIS CASTLE
From *The King's General*

Pendennis Castle plays a large part in *The King's General*, as the place to where the Prince's Council retreated. The castle is one of the finest fortresses built by Henry VIII and played a crucial role in the Civil War, being the last Royalist position in the West Country and the last castle to fall in England after a five month siege, under attack from land and sea. About 1,000 men, women and children surrendered because of starvation.

The King's General is set in 17th century Cornwall, and told by Honor Harris, whose Royalist family are fighting for the King against the Parliamentarians. "You will never see me wed to the man I love … but you will learn how that love never falters", she narrates, at the beginning of the novel.

This was Daphne's most complex plot so far, given that it involved a huge amount of history, with an entirely imaginary love story at the centre of it. The novel begins when eighteen year old Honor meets Richard Grenvile. He is a Colonel in the King's Army, knighted for gallant behaviour in the field, arrogant and quick witted, though his gallantry does not appear to extend to social occasions. Despite initial clashes and his being ten years older, they soon fall in love and become engaged. But the day before their wedding, Honor falls from her horse, and is in a coma, paralysed, so the wedding never takes place.

When she comes round, Honor decides not to see Richard again. He channels his ambition and love for Honor into his work, and rises through the ranks of the army, marrying another woman who bears his children. Meanwhile Honor remains in a wheelchair made by her brother, in her family home, and stays single.

The Civil War spreads throughout Cornwall, so Honor takes refuge at Menabilly, her sister and brother-in-law's home, where she meets Richard again for the first time in 15 years. His marriage is over and he has brought his 14 year old son, Dick, with him. Richard is now acting as the King's General in the West, in charge of the Royalist forces.

Richard makes it clear he still wants Honor, but she refuses him, showing him her twisted limbs. He is undeterred, but Honor feels that although he is very gentle towards her, he is at heart too cruel and ruthless. Despite finding that their love is as strong as ever, Honor refuses to marry him, feeling that he would come to resent her paralysis. She also fears that he is "First a soldier, second a lover", so she would always come second. Despite Honor refusing to marry him, their relationship grows throughout the book, withstanding war, rebellion and the many betrayals that surround them.

As the Parliamentarians advance, Richard Grenvile flees to Cornwall, having told the Prince's Council that the only way to save the west is to appoint a supreme commander (meaning himself). But Lord Hopton is appointed, and Richard is expected to serve under him, which he refuses to do. Richard is arrested on a charge of disloyalty and imprisoned at Launceston Castle.

Honor wishes to plead for his release to the Prince's Council which has moved to Pendennis Castle, and she persuades Richard's nephew, Jack, to get her an interview with the Prince of Wales.

Jack smuggles her into Pendennis Castle, where two servants carry her to a small tower and she meets the Prince of Wales, little more than a teenager, looking more like a gipsy than a prince. It had been agreed that if the Royalist forces were beaten, the Prince and his Council would escape to Scilly, while the rest of them held Pendennis against the rebel army. The Prince smiles and tells Honor that while he agrees Richard is the only person who could save the west, regrettably there is nothing that he, as Prince, can do. Honor replies that actually there is something he could do. When they set sail for Scilly, she asks that Richard be allowed to escape at the same time, and take a fishing boat to France.

Impressed by her loyalty to Richard, the Prince agrees to write a letter to Sir Arthur Basset at St Michael's Mount telling him that Richard should be free as soon as they sail for Scilly. When the Parliamentarians advance, the war in the West is lost, but at least Honor knows that her Richard is safe.

What you need to know	
Distance	2½ miles
Allow	1¼ hours
Suggested Map	OS Explorer 105 Falmouth & Mevagissey
Starting point	Pendennis Castle car park; grid reference SW 823321
Terrain	Easy going, few steep hills
Nearest refreshments	Ice cream vans Pendennis Point, Castle Beach cafe open summer only; Falmouth Hotel; Barrack Block cafe Pendennis Castle
Public transport	Falmouth Town Shuttle bus – Take the Pendennis Rise stop for circular route along seafront and the town centre. Runs all year round. Route 366 provided by OTS. More details at www.travelinesw.com Falmouth Docks railway station half a mile
Of interest	Pendennis Castle – www.english-heritage.org.uk/visit/places/pendennis-castle/prices-and-opening-times
Facilities	Pendennis Castle, Falmouth Hotel, and Public toilets along the seafront (seasonal)

Directions

Fiona and I followed the A39 to Pendennis Rise and Castle Drive which leads to the the designated car park for Pendennis Castle just past the Ships & Castles turning (post code TR11 4LP). Parking was free at time of walking, and we followed the signs to the castle – see website for opening hours and prices.

Pendennis Castle is a fort built by Henry VIII from 1540-42 to protect Falmouth and the Carrick Roads (river) against invasion from France and the Holy Roman Empire. At the end of the century the keep and gun platform were enlarged because of the increasing threat from the Spanish, and stone ramparts and bastions were built around the older castle. Pendennis was held by the Royalists in the Civil War and was finally taken by Parliament after a long siege in 1646. Charles II rebuilt the fortress when he was restored to the throne in 1660.

During the Napoleonic Wars, the castle held up to 48 guns, but in the 1880s and 1890s, new quick-firing guns were installed. The castle was in service in both World Wars but by 1956 it was obsolete and was decommissioned. It is now managed by English Heritage, and considered to be one of the finest examples of a post medieval defensive promontory fort in the country.

Once you've explored the castle, walk back the way you drove in, away from the Moat Walk, which goes round the inner area around the castle. Rather than walking along the road, we took a tarmac path on the left, past ox eye daisies showing their cheerful late summer faces, bindweed sprawling carelessly over various bushes, and the last of the blackberries. The sycamore trees were about to turn on this sunny morning in mid September.

By the sign that said Ships and Castles, we crossed the road and followed the sign on the right indicating Coastal footpath – Public Footpath, Pendennis Point ½ mile. We took the right hand fork through the woods, passing a huge toadstool that Fiona wasn't sure was edible, so we didn't risk it. This is a well trodden footpath, used by many dog walkers, and the road to Pendennis Castle and Point is up above on the right, while glimpses of the Carrick Roads could be seen on our left.

Sycamore trees formed a canopy over our heads, with ivy and rhododendron bushes on either side of us. After about five minutes the path comes up to

Ships near Pendennis Point

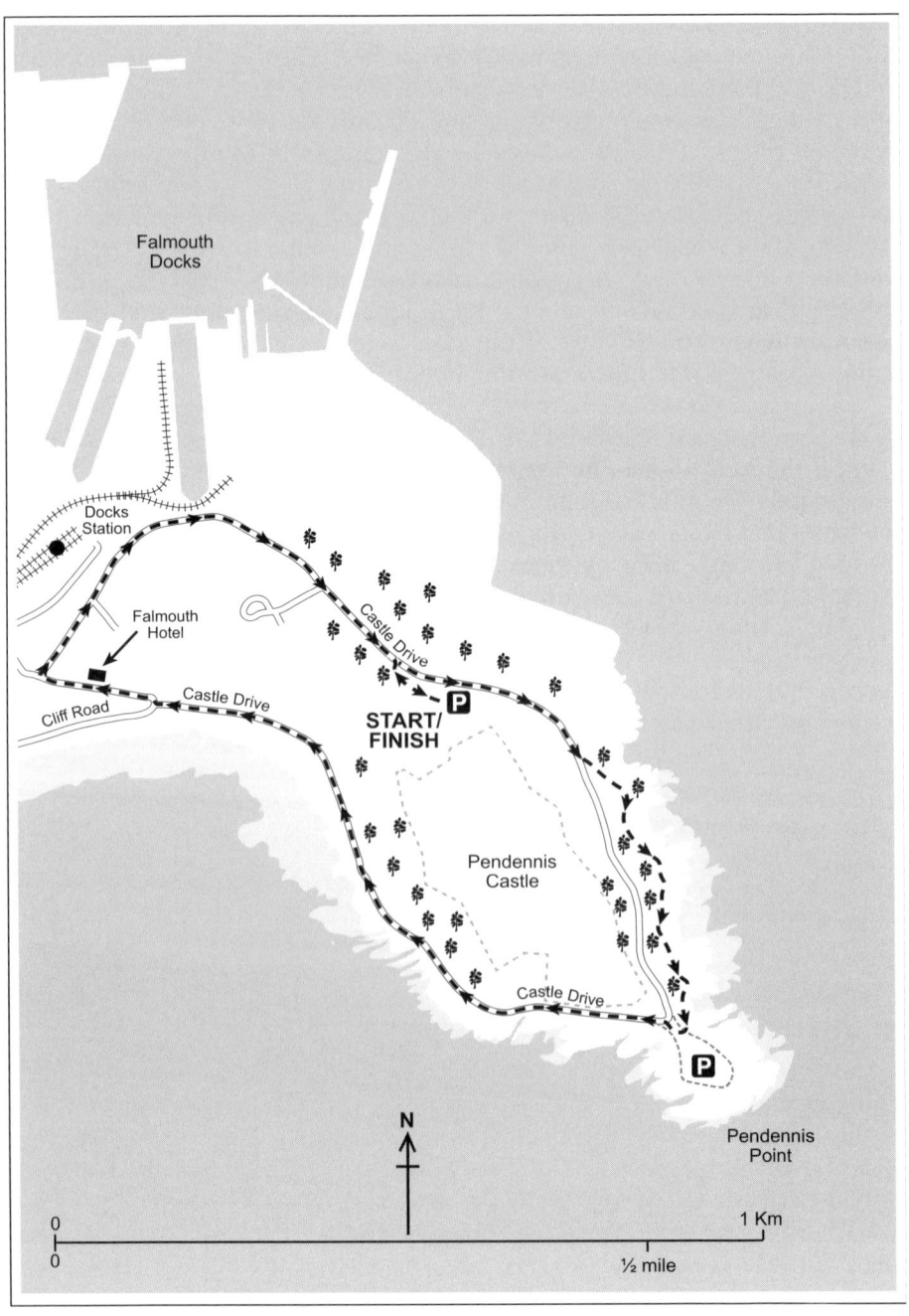

meet the road but we turned left past the driveway to a house and past a large tree decorated with floral tributes to some youngsters sadly killed in a car crash several years ago.

Just past here we had a clear view of Black Rock, the navigation mark that roughly divides the entrance of Falmouth harbour into two distinct channels; the eastern deep water channel and the western more shallow channel.

The story I like is that St Mawes, the tenth son of an Irish king, was busy preaching one day when he was interrupted by a seal, barking continuously. After a while he couldn't stand the noise any longer, and threw a huge rock at the seal. The rock missed but is still there today, wedged on top of a clump of black rocks halfway across the entrance to Falmouth harbour. The irony is that at low tide, seals often sunbathe on the rocks at the base of Black Rock – and presumably chuckling to themselves.

As we walked along, the Falmouth lifeboat chugged serenely out to sea, past a large black lugger drifting towards St Mawes, and we could see St Anthony's Lighthouse, and Lighthouse Beach, next door to it.

The sun glinted through the trees as we turned left onto an area housing several gun emplacements and a flat area popular with people having barbecues. The bracken was just starting to turn a pale brown, giving off a toasty smell in the sunshine.

It was a perfect moment to sit and drink in the warmth from the late summer sun, with the waves lapping gently below us. From here there are marvellous views up the Carrick Roads, over to St Mawes, and out into Falmouth Bay, where a selection of boats of all kinds sailed by: a little Mirror dinghy with a red sail, a leisure cruiser; a racing yacht, a white catamaran ; several tankers moored in the bay, and the distinctive blue St Mawes ferry trundling back and forth.

Leaving here, we looked left down to several unnamed small coves good for swimming and rocks which are very popular with fishermen. From here we continued uphill on the path which brought us to Pendennis Point. We went along the lower coastal path, with the Pendennis Point car park on our right, walking down to the keep of Little Dennis blockhouse, built at the same time as the castle itself, perched on the tip of Pendennis Point. The main gun port faces out across the estuary with another gun port facing out to sea.

Little Pendennis blockhouse

We continued walking westwards towards Gyllyngvase, looking towards Swanpool and Maenporth beaches: further down is Rosemullion Head, hiding the mouth of the Helford River. You can also see Dennis Head, which is the site of an iron age fort where the Royalists fell to the Parliamentarians at the end of the civil war in 1646.

If you happen to have binoculars you might be able to see the Coastguard Watch building at Nare Point. In the Second World War, Ealing Studios built a film set here as a decoy at night: when it was lit up it looked like Falmouth docks and the train depot. They did this with red and green coloured stop and go lights which would be visible from the cockpit of an incoming German bomber. This remotely controlled film set could mimic the light coming from an opening door and a poorly draped window. They also set off explosions to imitate trains being hit which encouraged the Germans to drop their bombs on the false Falmouth docks.

Looking even further west than Nare Point is Porthallow Beach and the dreaded Manacles rocks, where many ships have been wrecked. Manacles or Maen Eglos in Cornish means church rocks with reference to St Keverne's church where many of the drowned sailors were buried: on a clear day you can see the spire of this church.

Back at Pendennis, walking westwards round the Point you will come to various picnic benches, and in the car park above, several ice cream vans that also sell soup and hot drinks in winter. *Pinuccia*, the beautiful 8-metre classic yacht from the Tresanton Hotel in St Mawes glided by, as we walked into the car park then turned left, onto the pavement below Falmouth Coastguards Operation and Marine Office, a very important part of maritime services worldwide.

The Volunteer Coastguard Rescue Officers can be called out by the Maritime Rescue Co-ordination Centre (MRCC) at any time of the day or night, in all weathers, to respond to those in trouble or missing, to seek confirmation or further information of a report, or to participate in a joint response to an emergency.

Their duties involve: search for missing persons; rescuing those trapped or injured on cliffs or in mud; provide a limited water rescue capability; provide incident response and on-scene co-ordination and carry out accident prevention and safety education activities. In other words, for anyone in trouble on or near the sea, the Coastguards are the first people to turn to by dialling 999.

You can walk up the hill past the Coastguards and continue along the Moat Walk back to the Castle, but we continued walking along the lower pavement path, passing a bench with a man so deeply asleep that we stared at him as we crept past. "Do you think he's dead?" asked Fiona.

At that moment he looked up, so we breathed a sigh of relief, and continued past the huge satellite mast belonging to the Coastguards, up on our right, past the last of the sea campion and the bright red and yellow berries belonging to old man's beard.

A few cabbage white butterflies fluttered past, to the flap of Fiona's flip flops. On our right were steep, dense and mysterious woods with blackbirds tweeting from their depths. A public footpath takes you back through the trees to the castle, but we continued until we reached a car park on the left overlooking the sea, often used by diving schools.

Just before the car park we turned left and made our way down onto the rocks for a swim, but otherwise continue past the car park. Fiona's flip flops were squeaking by this time, as her feet were wet from her swim, and we looked up at various people enjoying picnics up on our right.

Further along here on the right is a small granite monument dedicated to Pendennis Motor Cycle and Light Car Club which commemorates the historic Pendennis Castle road races staged here 1931-1937. They were the first motorcycle races to be run on public roads in mainland Britain, with all proceeds going to the newly formed Falmouth hospital.

Continuing our way round towards the seafront, the big cream building of Falmouth Hotel loomed up ahead of us. There is also a cafe at Castle Beach, but this is seasonal, and was shut, so being in need of a snack, we headed along to the hotel where there is a sun trap of a terrace (or was today), where we relaxed with a coffee and, in my case, a very good fruit scone fresh out of the oven (or, cynically, microwave). When we went in to the bar to order the coffee, I noticed a blackboard advertising Thai Fish Curry. Somewhat mystifyingly, underneath it said, "contains no curry"....

Suitably refreshed, we came out of the hotel and turned left down the drive with tropical plants growing on either side. At the bottom of the drive is a small roundabout where we turned sharp right along Castle Hill which bears round to the left up Castle Drive. This takes you past Falmouth Docks with the dry dock of A&P below on the left, and Pendennis Shipyard's massive ship building halls, famous for building and restoring superyachts worldwide.

Cove near Little Pendennis

On our right, looking inland, we noticed a concrete shed with a beautiful wall of graffiti saying, "I miss my little brother", which brought a sobering note to the morning. Continuing up the hill, we crossed the road and arrived back at the Ships & Castle's turning, where we retraced our steps along the tarmac path and thereby back to the car park.

It's fascinating to wander round the castle and keep and I am glad it is still used, even if not for its original purpose. I have attended a wedding and various singing events in the keep which has a cosy, intimate air to it. And picturing the inside of the keep, I can see Honor, shaking with nerves before her audience with the Prince of Wales, desperate to save the man she so dearly loves.

Reading this part of the novel, set in the castle, I am glad to note that the Prince of Wales, also an admirer of Richard, is very taken by Honor's courage and support of him. The Prince smiles slowly, saying that Richard is most fortunate to have such a faithful ally. "If I am ever in his shoes, and find myself a fugitive, I hope I can rely on half so good a friend."

Along with many other dog walkers, I often walk round the castle moat, as our dogs chase squirrels, rabbits, magpies – sometimes a fox. It is a beautiful, unexpected corner of Falmouth, with the castle rising serenely in the middle, silhouetted against the sky. It always makes me think of Honor's bravery, and the desperate fight of Richard Grenvile and the Royalists.

I came to this book comparatively recently and was struck by the unusual main characters: an arrogant, insensitive alpha male who cares nothing of what other people think, and a strong minded, independent woman trapped by her circumstances. Yet when they meet, there is true love and a meeting of two clever minds, which is obviously important to Du Maurier. Her earlier short stories were full of woman badly treated by men, so it is cheering to meet Honor, a woman who very much knows her own mind, stands up to the man she loves, yet fights for him in her own way, as he fights to be with her – when he can. This might not be one of her most famous novels, but it is a fascinating and very moving read.

WALK TEN
FRENCHMAN'S CREEK - HELFORD
The setting for the novel

This is one of my favourite parts of Cornwall, first brought to my attention as a teenager, reading *Frenchman's Creek*, inspired by the pirates and free traders who worked these waters during the Napoleonic wars. Many years ago Helford was an important port where trading ships brought rum, port, tobacco and lace from the continent. Those days are long gone, the houses mostly holiday homes, but du Maurier's descriptions of the Helford River are so vivid, you can still identify this magical, secretive part of Cornwall.

Daphne and her new husband, Tommy Browning, came here on his boat for their honeymoon in 1932, and she loved it. It was, "completely captivating; never had I experienced such a tranquil setting", she said.

However, some locals believe that the creek is haunted by evil spirits. Many years ago, an old man took a short cut across the creek, but didn't get home that night. His body was found the following morning, sitting upright in the river, his hat still on his head, and his long white beard trailing in the water. Locals believe that his spirit still lingers in the cottages around the Helford area.

In 1940, Daphne was in the grip of post natal depression following the birth of her longed-for son, Christian (Kit). She was also strongly attracted to Christopher Puxley, in whose house she had been staying, in Hertfordshire. She was sick of the war, found her husband exhausted and bad tempered whenever he came back on leave, and Daphne's thoughts wandered to Cornwall, where she longed to be out on their boat. She dreamed of battles, and storms at sea and into her head came the idea of an educated, artistic pirate (who closely resembled Christopher Puxley) who tempted the heroine away from the husband she no longer loved.

The book very much echoed the emotions that Daphne was battling with at the time. She was happier with Christopher than with her husband, but she had a strong sense of duty and knew she would never leave Tommy, whom she still loved. Fugitives, and escapism, play a big part in du Maurier's novels – perhaps because she was always trying to escape, and only ever found peace when she was writing.

She says that this is the only one of her novels that she admits is romantic, but she wanted it to be more than that: she wanted to evoke the sense of history, mystery and enchantment of Frenchman's Creek. Sir Arthur Quiller-Couch used the title as one of his short stories but told Daphne she could use it.

This book remains one of my favourite Daphne du Maurier books. She wrote it in 1941, setting it in the reign of Charles II. A sense of location was very strong for her, as is evident in the first chapter. "When the east wind blows up Helford river the shining waters become troubled and disturbed, and the little waves beat angrily upon the sandy shores. The short seas break above the bar at ebb-tide, and the waders fly inland to the mud flats, their wings skimming the surface, and calling to one another as they go."

Lady Dona St Columb, tired of London's high society and her boring husband, escapes to Cornwall, taking her two young children and their nurse to stay at Navron, her husband's estate on the river Helford. Once there she revels in the freedom of a Cornish summer. Her peace is disturbed by a neighbour, Lord Godolphin, who tells of a French pirate who has been seizing goods, robbing estates and escaping before the Cornish gentry can catch him. Godolphin wants Dona to ask her husband to come to Cornwall so they can outwit the pirate, but Dona is enjoying her time alone and ignores his request.

Exploring the woods one day, she comes across a creek hidden from the main river Helford, and sees a ship hiding there at anchor. She is taken aboard and finds it is the French pirate's ship. But he is not the vicious ruffian she expected; he's an attractive, intelligent philosopher with a talent for sketching wild birds. He is also a fugitive from his empty life as an aristocrat in France, and enjoys the challenge of capturing the cargoes of English merchant ships on their return to Cornwall.

When they meet, they are instantly drawn to each other, recognising kindred spirits. He teaches her to fish and light a fire. Later, she dresses up as his cabin boy and joins him, plundering a ship that belongs to one of her own neighbours. But things don't go according to plan, and the Frenchman is arrested, due to be hanged the following day. Unless Dona can come up with a rescue plan ...

What you need to know	
Distance	3½ miles
Allow	2 hours
Suggested Map	OS Explorer 103 The Lizard, Falmouth and Helston
Starting point	Helford car park, behind Ferryboat Inn; grid ref: SW 764270
Terrain	Steep in places
Nearest refreshments	Ferryboat Inn, Shipwrights Inn
Helford Ferry	Check seasonal running times on www.helford-river-boats.co.uk/ferry
Public transport	OTS 323 bus from Helston and Mullion stops at the Helford car park. Ring 08712002233 for bus times
Of interest	Frenchman's Creek, Kestle Barton – www.kestlebarton.co.uk
Facilities	Ferryboat Inn, Shipwrights Inn and public toilets at car park at Helford Village

Directions

One sultry afternoon, Deb, Viv, MollieDog, Titch (Moll's boyfriend) and I met in Falmouth and drove along Hillhead Road to Penwarne Road, which led to Sampys Hill in Mawnan Smith. In the village we followed signs to Glendurgan and Trebah Gardens, then straight on to the Ferryboat Inn. Nearing the bottom of the hill is a car park on the right where you can park all day for a pound at time of walking. We then walked the remainder of the way down to Helford Passage and waited for the passenger ferry (£6 return for adults) on the beach outside the Ferryboat Inn.

With a brisk north easterly blowing, the pontoon was bucking like a nervous horse, and, while Deb is used to boats, Viv paled. "Are you sure about this?"

she said. Trying to still my stomach, heaving along with the waves, I nodded and clambered into the little passenger ferry as it tossed and turned alongside. Viv gulped, picked up Titch and hurried on board. Thankfully that was the difficult bit – by the time we reached Helford Point opposite, it was more sheltered, and Viv and Titch were looking decidedly less hangdog.

Much cheered by reaching dry land, we walked along the path towards Helford Village with time to appreciate the sun sparkling like jewels on the river. A settlement was first recorded here in 1230, and it is thought the ferry and ford date from then. There are also records of medieval oyster beds in the river. Heading through the village past the Shipwrights Inn, we continued to a footbridge over a stream, and on reaching a row of whitewashed cottages, turned right up a Public Footpath sign saying 'Manaccan ¾ mile'. After a short distance the lane continued past a thatched cottage and into woods where the sun danced through the trees, dappling the leaves with an intense white light.

We followed the path as it forked right westwards over a stream, over a small granite stile up through the woods and into a field. At the top of this field, we came to Kestle Barton, which describes itself as a rural centre for contemporary arts. It was built in 17th century, on a mediaeval site first documented in 1300. The converted farmstead now houses a gallery where an exhibition was being hung so we went in to have a look. Next to the gallery

Kestle farmhouse

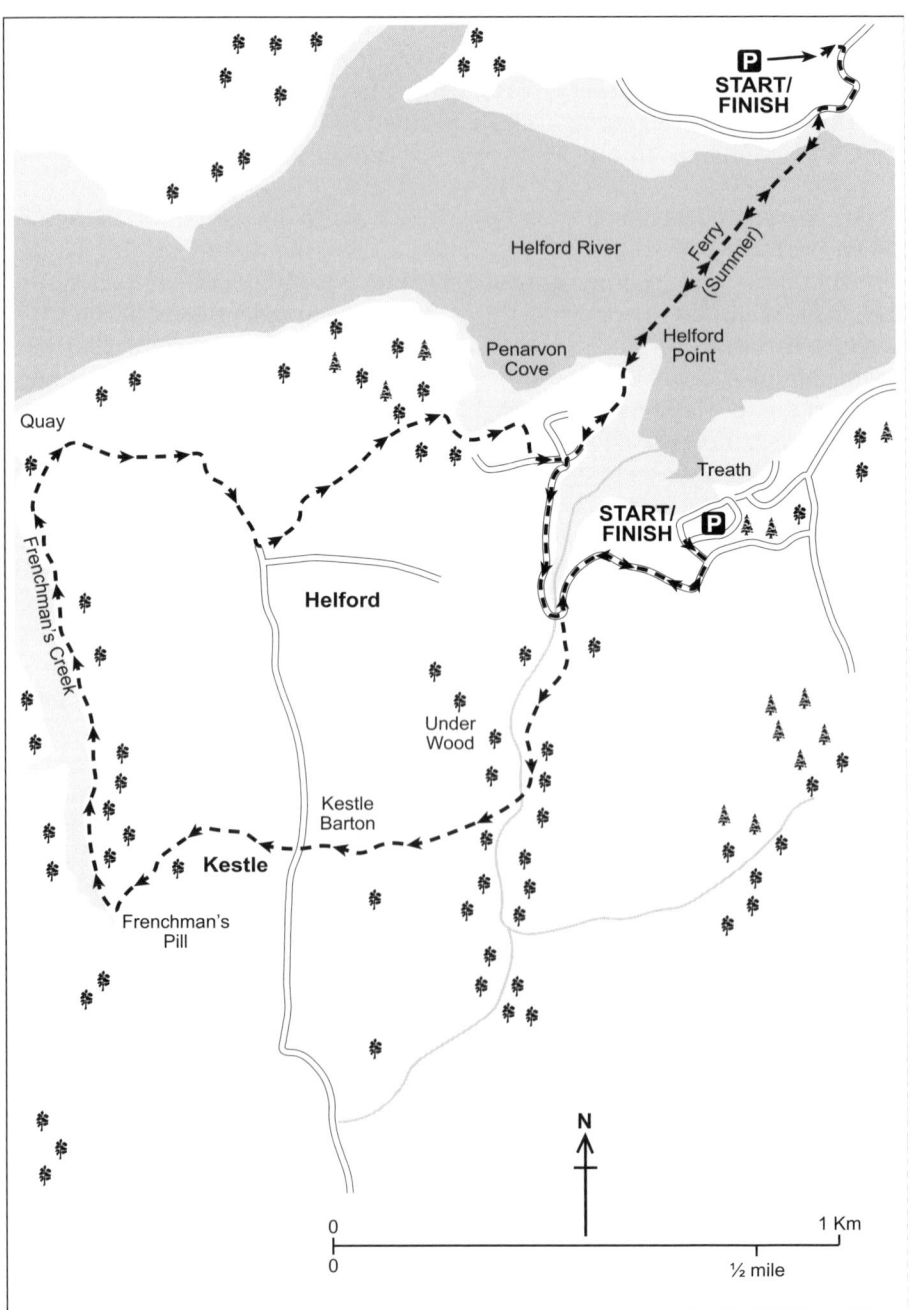

is a self service refreshment area, so we sat and ate local ice cream sitting on the benches outside, while admiring the beautiful rambling garden, full of purple Verbena and brilliant yellow Rudbekia, and the wild meadow beyond. The surrounding barns and the old farmhouse have all been converted into holiday accommodation: a perfect place for a secluded getaway.

From here we crossed the road, following a Public Footpath sign over a granite stile into a path beside a lush grassy field on our left where three trees, several feet high, had been planted at random points. We pondered this while rooks cawed above us, and we passed through a wooden gate and on our right, a seat made of a huge slab of granite. Above the tall hedges we could make out an orchard on our right as we headed down into the woods, past chubby rose hips and banks of unripe blackberries.

The rough lane had diagonal stones acting as gullies to channel the water that must run through the woods – a sensible precaution in these times of abundant rain. Despite not having had much rain for a while, the woods felt damp and dark, slender trees jostling for position, throttled with ivy. We passed a huge old oak tree with the trunk split in half, smothered in thick moss; further up its ivy coated branches, bracken sprouted like tufts of hair.

Coming to a fork in the path we followed a sign on the right indicating Frenchman's Creek (Permissive Path) and headed even further downhill. "Hmm", muttered Viv. "What goes down must come up." But at that moment we reached the creek and all thoughts of steep hills were forgotten.

Frenchman's Creek is a secretive, silent place, redolent with the sense of times gone by. Du Maurier, describes the first time Dona comes across the creek: "There before her was the creek, still and soundless, shrouded by the trees, hidden from the eyes of men. The tide was ebbing, the water oozing away from the mud flats, and here, where she stood, was the head of the creek itself for the stream ended in a trickle, and the trickle in a spring."

The dogs danced along by the mud while we stopped and just looked. At low tide the creek is littered with massive rotting trees, like felled giants, draped in seaweed; a lone egret stalked through a mud bank while rooks cawed above. Our chatter must have disturbed the wildlife, for a pigeon cooed in the trees and curlews cried eerily as they flew over the river. A narrow trickle of water wound its way down the creek in an 'S' shape to where a grey heron stood, still and silent as a statue.

Mouth of creek low tide

The dogs had a wonderful time hurtling through the trees, and as we walked along the narrow, twisty path, it was easy to imagine Dona St Columb, pausing as she saw a strange ship at anchor, moored in the creek, heard a sound of tapping and hammering, then a burst of French singing. Here Viv burst into something she sang at school which involved 'sabots' but was probably not sung by French pirates.

We passed over three footbridges, and by a tree on the left, we took the right fork which led up some steps then followed the Creekside Path on the left, which did just that, passing round the end of the creek, where we had a wonderful view of the two old quays of traditional Cornish stone, the Helford river shimmering before us, and the final resting place of an old, abandoned boat. Out in the open we inhaled the toasty smell of sun baked bracken and picked blackberries that smelt of candyfloss, and gave us claret stained fingers. We continued along here until we reached a tarmac path where we headed right uphill with a field on the left. This field was edged with a strip of grass from which ox eye daisies and lush clover grew in abundance, and the last of the honeysuckle and rose hips peeked forth from the hedges.

Ahead of us a group of pine trees were silhouetted against the sky as we climbed up the top of this steep hill, where we found a conveniently placed bench, today occupied by people having a picnic. Both dogs rushed over hoping to share their food (no luck) and we joined the picnickers for one last look back across Helford River. On past here, we turned right along a track signed Penarvon Cove, crossed a submerged cattle grid and turned left signed to Pengweden and Helford.

Pigeons cooed above us, while blackbirds tweeted noisily from the trees as we headed down this lane, passing another tree covered in bouncy ivy, like an afro hairstyle. Coming to a fork we continued downhill until we reached Penarvon Cove, an idyllic spot with several picturesque National Trust cottages being repainted, accompanied by the tinny tunes of Neil Sedaka coming from a tiny radio hung on a wall.

We sat on a log here while Viv ate her pasty (my sandwich was long gone) and as we stretched our legs in the sunshine, real life responsibilities seemed a long way away. Tiny fish performed nautical acrobatics in the water, spreading tiny ripples as we watched, while we sat and drank in the peace and tranquillity of this precious little cove.

Following the Public Footpath sign back through the woods, we climbed away from the cove, through a metal gate at the top, until we reached a steep path leading downhill to the left, back into Helford Village, by the Shipwrights Inn. This is well worth a visit, and we sat outside, overlooking the creek, lapping up a beer with the last of the late summer sunshine.

View out to the estuary

From here we turned left to get the passenger ferry back to Helford Passage. It was such a lovely afternoon that we wandered along to the private (dog friendly) beach at the end, where we sat and planned our next walk while the dogs nosed contentedly up and down the beach.

"You know, this part of Cornwall reminds me that I'm just an insignificant walker", said Viv. "I have no rights to this beautiful place, but feel so lucky to be able to pass through, enjoy it, and leave it undisturbed. I only hope it stays like this for the next few hundred years."

Frenchman's Creek is still a magic place, and I hope it will always remain so. But the last word must go to the writer herself. "(The solitary yachtsman) is alone and yet – can that be a whisper, in the shallows, close to the bank, and does a figure stand there, the moonlight glinting upon his buckled shoes and the cutlass in his hand, and is that a woman by his side, a cloak around her shoulders, her dark ringlets drawn back behind her ears?"

In 1989 the Ferryboat Inn at Helford Passage was involved as the centre of a smuggling ring, importing drugs such as cocaine and marijuana. When Daphne heard about this she apparently said, "I'm not interested in the little people who get caught, but in those who really run it, the ring. Now, if I were to set a drugs ring in an old Cornish house, then perhaps we'd have the start of another novel".

WALK ELEVEN
TRELOWARREN - THE HALLIGGYE WALK
The estate that inspired Navron, in *Frenchman's Creek*

"The most beautiful place imaginable – a shock of surprise, a delight, lying indeed like a jewel in the hollow of a hand", is how Du Maurier described Trelowarren in her diary after her first visit there with Foy Quiller-Couch, to meet Clara Vyvyan. Clara was 45 when she and Daphne, aged 23, first met in 1929, shortly after the publication of *The Loving Spirit*.

Four years before, Clara and a friend plus two guides crossed from Canada to Alaska collecting and pressing wild flowers for Kew Gardens. She loved being outside; travelled to Ireland where she slept on a newspaper, paddled a canoe down river in Alaska; explored the mangrove swamps of Australia and walked along the Rhone from its glacier source to the Mediterranean delta. Nature was her sanctuary and she was very adept at describing it, along with her precious plants. As well as her travel books, which are still very popular, she also wrote *A Cornish Year*, *Roots and Stars* and *Our Cornwall*, several volumes of autobiography and a novel.

I was fortunate enough to meet Victoria Vyvyan who told me more about the friendship between Clara and Daphne. "Clara Vyvyan was my husband's great-aunt", says Victoria. "She wasn't a Vyvyan herself - she married Courtenay Vyvyan, who lived at Trelowarren."

Trelowarren is the most impressive estate, and has belonged in the Vyvyan family for the last six hundred years. "You come in through either of the gates and because of the happy coincidence of the house being in the middle of the estate, you get a real sense of getting away from the world", Victoria tells me.

She has given various talks on the relationship between Clara and Daphne, at the Du Maurier Festival in Fowey (now the Fowey Festival) and the Ways with

Words festival in Dartington, Devon. "The central premise was that they had a terrific amount in common even though they were separated by many years. They were both intelligent women who should have gone to university and they were both denied that by restrictive Victorian parenting", Victoria explains. "Clara's mother was a Willliams from Caerhays so that's where her love of plants came from."

But it wasn't just their backgrounds that brought them together. "I think they were alike in their writing – they both worked hard at it, but were essentially in the Romantic tradition, of spontaneity and intensity and reaction to landscape. I think they both sublimated their own frustrations in their writing – in a passion for place and travel, and I think they were quite supportive of each other."

Daphne would often stay at Trelowarren, and saw it as her refuge. Which was why she based Navron, the house in *Frenchman's Creek*, on Trelowarren, although those wishing to retrace her steps down to the river will be disappointed. There are no public rights of way through the estate to the water, and looking at the map, there are no paths along the river from Tremayne Quay towards Helford, so Du Maurier used a certain amount of artistic licence in her descriptions in the book.

Being at Trelowarren, and in particularly staying here, it's easy to see why Daphne loved it so much. "Staying in the houses and being on Trelowarren are synonymous", says Victoria. "We want people to stay here so they can really appreciate what it's about. The houses are luxurious but it's part of a whole – being part of something that has been here for such a long time. It's about leaving the world behind, and seeing this as a refuge."

What you need to know	
Distance	1½ miles
Allow	1 hour
Suggested Map	OS Explorer 103 Falmouth, Helston and Lizard
Starting point	New Yard restaurant; grid reference SW 721239
Terrain	Easy going
Nearest refreshments	New Yard restaurant, Trelowarren

Public transport	Bus to Helston; taxi from there
Of interest	Clock and clock tower, turret, the Mount, Iron Age Fort and Fogou, Venton Gannell cottages and Restoration Gates
Facilities	Toilets at the yard, Trelowarren

Directions

From Helston take the A3083 south towards Culdrose and The Lizard. Just past Culdrose, turn left at the mini roundabout onto the B3293 to Goonhilly/St Keverne. At the top of the hill (Mawgan Cross roundabout) take the third exit (do NOT go into Mawgan village) drive past Garras Primary School and just round the corner take the left turn signed to Trelowarren. Drive down the slip road and in, right, through the gates and follow signs to the New Yard restaurant.

The permissive paths on Trelowarren are not Rights of Way and are open from February 1st to September 30th only. Please keep dogs on leads.

One mizzly afternoon in June, Viv and I parked in the main car park near the New Yard restaurant and decided to have a look around. Heading towards the yard, we walked through a wooden door, past wrought iron pergolas from

New Yard

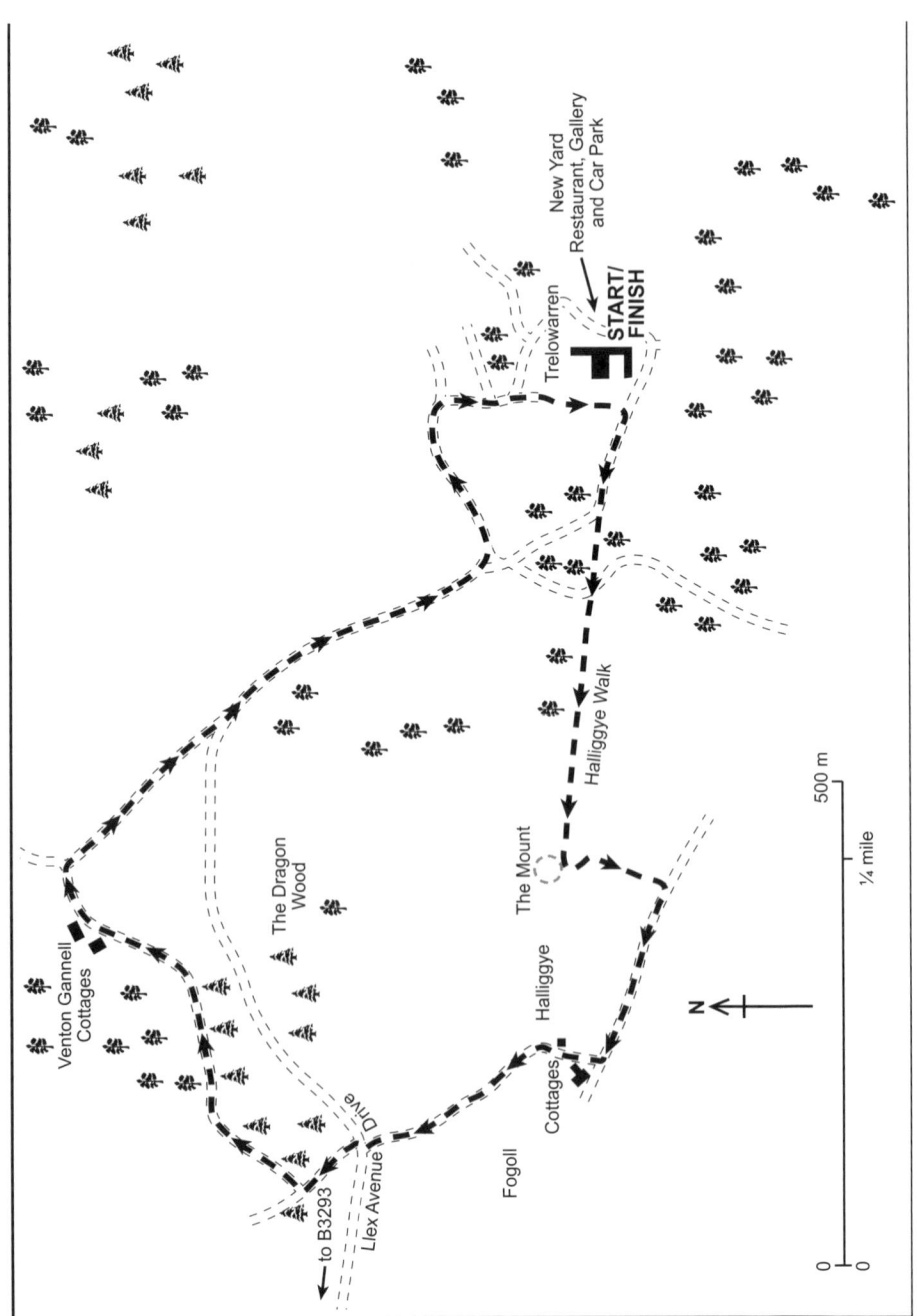

which pale pink roses climbed in and around, a stone mounting block, and into the yard, where we found the New Yard restaurant. There is also a gallery here and a pizza venue, which we visited on another occasion, but for this walk we left the yard at the top right, by the old tack room which is now the toilets.

Keeping the walled garden on the right, we walked along to the main car park looking back at the clock and clock tower. The Trelowarren clock can be heard chiming all over the estate but in the 1970s it was stolen to order. It was taken first to Sweden and then to an antique shop in Belgium where it was seen by one of the Vyvyans who brought it home. To celebrate its return, Virginia Vyvyan decided to completely restore the tower which has an elderly but effective wind vane. This was used by GIs as target practice in the run up to D-Day, hence the spattering of holes in its tail.

Walking past some plum trees on the red brick wall, we marvelled at the way the plums have been espaliered into each recess to provide beautiful blossom: sweet fruit grows on the south facing walls of this garden and the naturally sour fruit trees on the north and east walls.

We also noted apple and fig trees and walked along until we came to a crenellated turret which is part of the folly wall running along the drive to the house, which was altered in the 18th century.

Walking through the turret, we came to a smaller car park with a sign and a blue sign indicating Halliggye. Through the car park, we headed out through the other side and over a granite stile, then across the drive and followed the right hand hedge of a large field to the Mount. The edge of this field has a path mown

Chapel at Trelowarren

119

around the edge of it for walkers and to protect wild life – we saw several butterflies and masses of brambles which, as well as providing good blackberries, provide good nesting grounds for songbirds.

Above the multitudinous brambles were oak and sycamore trees, which form part of the wind break for the garden, while on our left, to the south, we could see the Goonhilly satellite dishes, wind turbines that emerged spookily from the low cloud, turning lazily in the light wind, and more and more woodland, wherever we looked.

At the end of this field we found the Mount on our right, looking ancient and mysterious though it is actually formed from the spoil of the new drive. It is the highest point on the Lizard and from here you can see the Western Approaches and the Channel.

Having explored the Mount and admired the stunning views, even when swathed in low cloud, we crossed a granite cattle grid and saw a coffin-rest on our left. Many years ago, coffins had to be carried across fields to the nearest graveyard, so these rest ledges are often found throughout the countryside.

The sun tried to break through as we followed a path on the left hand side of the field through patches of clover, buttercups and Alexander, and hedges full of campion and bindweed, with the last of the foxgloves waving tall in the breeze. As we walked, we smelt the beautifully sweet, pungent scent of camomile beneath our feet, and at the end of this field we turned right into a farm track.

At the end of this track we saw some beautiful cottages, lovingly restored, among hedges of dog roses and ox eye daisies. We turned right before we got to them, and walked past other fairytale cottages, whispering as we passed: they seemed almost out of this world – how wonderful to stay in one of those!

At the end of this drive is a stunning panoramic view of the countryside – the woodlands spreading out, enigmatic and dark, a few isolated cottages and a tapestry of fields with gently curving boundaries. Turning left we walked up a few slate steps into the Fogou – a Cornish word meaning 'cave'. These are only found in the far west of Cornwall and may have been used to store food or as a refuge in times of conflict. Their original function isn't clear, but they may also have been used for ceremonies or rituals. This particular fogou provides ideal conditions for the hibernation of the rare greater horseshoe bat, which needs to be undisturbed while hibernating, so the fogou is closed in the winter.

The Halliggye Iron Age fort is a scheduled Ancient Monument and one of the oldest examples of its kind in Northern Europe. All sorts of amazing tales are associated with this series of underground tunnels and spaces but the most reliable source of information is probably the Scheduled Ancient Monument listing. It was apparently used during the Second World War by the Manaccan Auxiliary Unit as an explosives and ammunition store.

Coming out of the fogou – which is very dark, and can be slippery inside, so take a torch and wear shoes with good grip – we were greeted by a profusion of elderflower blossom. Turning right, we headed down the drive just as the sun burst out, highlighting the sculpted edges of the fields – there are no straight lines to be seen, just sinuous curves leading to another mystical view, and long grass rippling in the wind.

Crossing the drive we noted the Ilex avenue – this is the botanical name for the Mediterranean oaks planted here in the 19th century, although they look much older. The trees were heavily pollarded but the winter storms of 2014 did a lot of damage – not that this was noticeable. As the sun glinted through the trees, you could see that this would be even more stunning in the evening sun.

After about 25 yards we turned right through Dragon Wood while pigeons cooed in the trees, and we thought we heard a peacock in the distance but we could have been wrong. Passing mossy banks and very old beech and sycamore trees, you could see and almost feel how old these dense woods are. A huge old oak tree was felled – by nature – revealing massive roots, while tendrils of ivy hung from the other trees.

Soon we came to Venton Gannell cottages, the first of which is on a little island with a device to keep the water flowing past it rather than through it. The second is a real gingerbread cottage: thatched with roses growing up the outside and a dracaena palm outside for the Cornish touch. These cottages were built in 1790, so not as old as they might seem, but still beautiful to look at and, I would imagine, to stay in.

At the end of this drive we came to a field on the right named Great Tregenna and walked up through here (cattle at the time of walking) along a track that

Venton Gannel cottages

leads back to the drive. Looking round, we could see miles of dense woodland and a field of intense emerald green – a wonderful contrast to the darkness of the woods.

From here we turned left and came across the Restoration Gates which were commissioned by the Royalist Vyvyans to celebrate the Stuart restoration and placed in front of the house. After the failure of the Bonnie Prince Charlie rebellion in 1745, the gates were moved to their current location to signify that the family were backing the Hanoverians.

Finally we made our way back along the drive accompanied by swooping swallows, and we kept a look out for the very popular goldfinches which abound here. Rewarding ourselves with a very good cup of coffee at the New Yard restaurant, we pondered the magnificence of this estate. As Victoria Vyvyan said, this is a carefully designed landscape, not a natural one, and needs a huge amount of maintenance. Many things are not as they seem: the fogou is very old but the Mount is not. The Ilex avenue seems old but is part of the new drive.

"A designed landscape is a stage set. It's not an accident that when you drive here you get a sense of being drawn into something mysterious. We have mysterious edges, so when you come in across the park fields it doesn't look like a traditional park. All the field boundaries are these beautiful undulating curves and coming up the Ilex avenue, there are these curves so the drive is always leading your eye into a mystifying future and a sense of an event."

Another draw of the place is that it is really very ancient. "People have lived here for so many thousands of years", adds Victoria. "The fogou is the longest continuously inhabited place in Europe. It's fabulously ancient in itself but people have always lived there – it's not just another abandoned hill fort. So you get a sense of the past here and I think that makes it feel very safe and secluded."

No wonder Daphne du Maurier was so spellbound by the place. I can picture her walking the grounds with her beloved dogs and Clara, earnestly discussing her latest novel, or Clara's latest book, both at home in the outdoors, exchanging views and confiding in each other. What better place than this magical, mystical estate that is so much a part of the past yet is careful to look to the future as well.

WALK TWELVE
LOE BAR/POOL

The setting for the end of *Frenchman's Creek*

By the end of the novel, Dona is a changed woman. Because of the Frenchman, she has tasted true adventure, she has killed the dreadful Rockingham in self defence, and she knows what it is to truly love, and be loved in return. For the first time in both their lives, Dona and the Frenchman have experienced a meeting of minds as well as bodies.

When he is captured and accused of murder, Dona does her utmost to save her lover from being hanged. She sends her husband and children back to London and, knowing she only has 24 hours to save her pirate, forms a highly dangerous plan, involving her faithful servant, William, who impersonates a doctor who has helped Lady Godolphin give birth. Du Maurier's mischievous sense of humour shows when he is asked how heavy the baby was. Four pounds, he hazards. Then realising that was wrong, opts for fifteen or sixteen pounds …

Despite this and other hiccups, Dona and William manage to release the Frenchman from the tower in which he is imprisoned. While William goes to secure a boat, Dona and the Frenchman ride fast to Loe Bar to discuss their future – for he must escape as he is to be hanged the following day.

Daphne's affair with Christopher Puxley lasted for many years, but she knew that she would never leave her husband, and never told Christopher that she would. But Christopher was less pragmatic than the French pirate, who knew that they had no future: only the present, and accepted the time they had together as something special that could not last. Whereas Christopher longed for more.

While I always cry at the end of this book – because they do not get together – I see that it may not have worked. How could she abandon her children?

How could he become absorbed in the domestics of her life when that was what they were both trying to escape? But was their love not strong enough?

The biggest problem her publishers, Victor Gollancz, had, was how to get enough paper to print the novel on. Paper was in short supply, given wartime restrictions. Despite that, they managed a print run of 50,000 copies.

What you need to know	
Distance	4 miles approximately
Allow	2¼ hours including stop for refreshments
Suggested Map	OS Explorer 103 The Lizard, Falmouth and Helst
Starting point	Penrose Hill car park; grid reference SW 639259
Terrain	Fairly flat but uneven
Nearest refreshments	Stables cafe open 10-4 all week in summer: check for opening times in winter
Public transport	Bus 234 Porthleven to Helston
Parking	At Penrose Estate car park £2 donation at time of walking
Of interest	Loe Bar and Loe Pool Helston History – www.helstonhistory.co.uk/loe-bar-pool/loe-bar/
Facilities	Toilets at Stables cafe

Directions

From Helston take Five Wells Lane to Monument Road, then follow the B3304 towards Porthleven until you reach a steep bend. Penrose Estate National Trust car park, which can be very busy at high season, is signposted off on the left. Parking £2 donation at time of walking.

Leaving the car park, southward and therefore seaward, Viv and Titch, Carol, Pilot, MollieDog and I headed down a little path with a gate at the end, which led to a wooden signpost on the right indicating 'Loe Pool ¾km 15 minutes. Stables 20 minutes. Helston 50 minutes'.

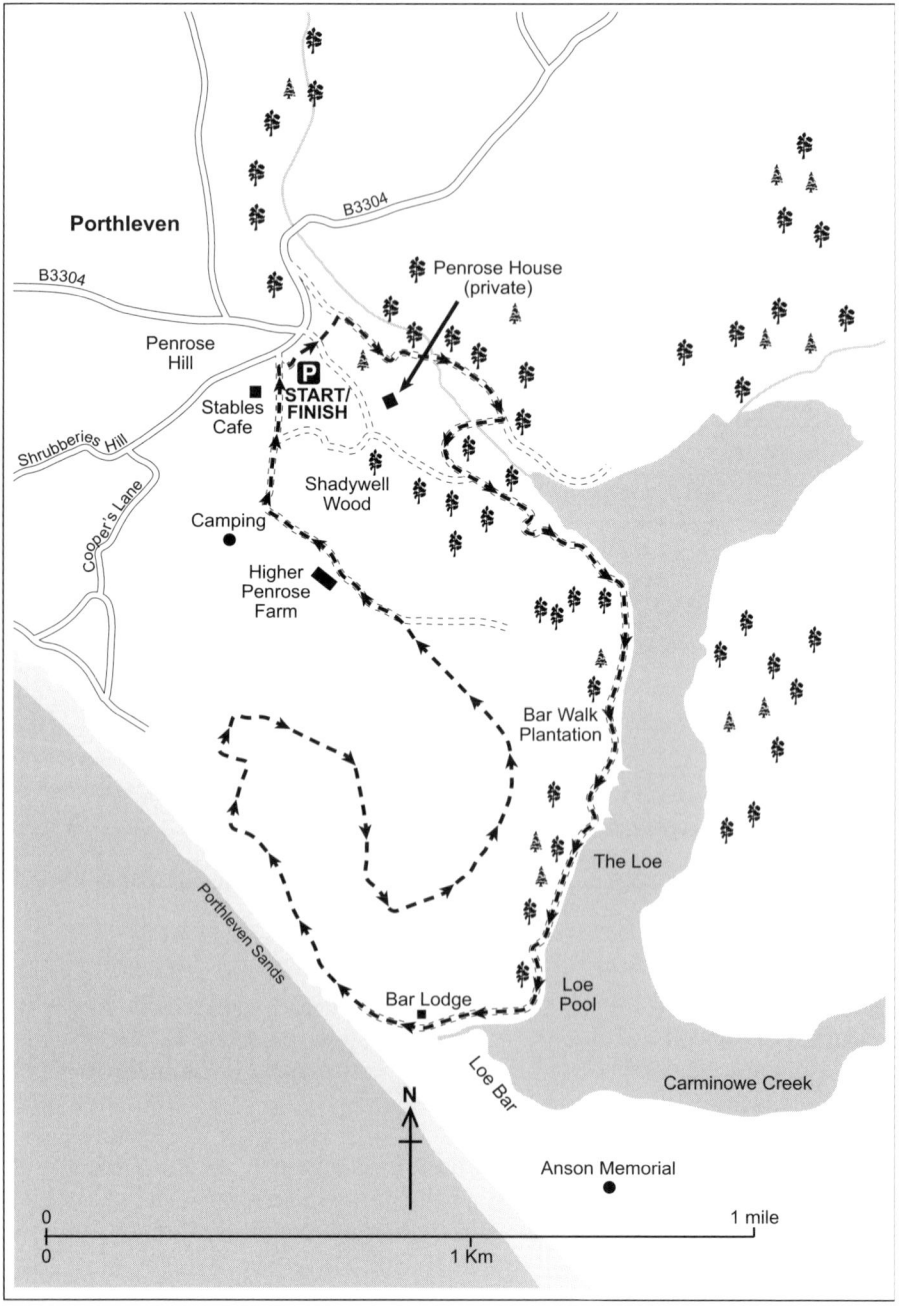

We headed down the hill through the trees, down some steep steps and continued, turning right, towards the sign to the Stables. Walking past some magnificent old oak trees and the Penrose Estate on our left, with iron railings marking the boundary to the estate, it looks like something out of a Jane Austen novel with elegant green parkland, a few grazing sheep and cattle, and the aforementioned oak trees supervising it all.

Since mediaeval times, the Penrose family have owned a large estate that extended from Gunwalloe to Porthleven Harbour. Penrose House was created in the 17th century but refurbished several times in the 18th and 19th centuries. 1,500 acres was gifted to the National Trust in 1974.

The tarmac drive winds round in front of Penrose House and walled garden, until we reached the Stables cafe, which has limited seating inside, but lots of picnic style benches outside, supplies good coffee and excellent sandwiches and cake. The walled kitchen garden next door is also worth a visit, where all kinds of vegetables in season are grown – rhubarb, courgettes, beans and peas when we had a look.

Leaving the Stables cafe, we noted a map on the wall of the Penrose Trails – there are several – but the route we opted for goes through Shadywalk Wood to Loe Bar, then continues along the coastal path towards Porthleven, and takes a route inland back to the car park.

Stables courtyard

The path continues along with Loe Pool on our left, just visible through the summer foliage of the trees, then through a very dense part of the woods. It is very popular for family outings, as we passed many groups with children and dogs, cycling, running and walking.

Grey squirrels are abundant, having been brought here from the USA in the late 19th century. They bred so rapidly that within decades they had replaced the native red squirrel in most parts of the UK, being larger so they can survive colder winters, and are better suited to urbanisation.

Throughout the wood, the National Trust has introduced keep fit areas – we came across a stepping beam: part of a Green Gym, which is all about using woodland walks to get fitter. This particular area consisted of stumps of different heights, the purpose being to get round the course without touching the ground. "Or breaking your ankle", observed Viv, who broke hers last year – though not, I hasten to add, by attempting any part of the Green Gym. You'd need long legs, however, as the stumps were quite a long way apart: enough to put both of us off.

There are a lot of sweet chestnut trees growing around Loe Pool; a tree from Sardinia that was introduced into Britain by the Romans to provide food for their troops. Peeking through the trees, down to the Pool, we spotted a heron: grey herons have a six foot wingspan and are usually seen in or near freshwater. Although they eat mostly fish, they also prey on frogs, moles, ducklings, rodents and even baby rabbits. In Tudor and Elizabethan times, herons were hunted with peregrine falcons as a royal sport.

We also saw a few swans on the lake. These birds usually mate for life, though a nesting failure can be grounds for divorce. Swans often live for over twenty years but in the 20th century many of these birds got lead poisoning from the lead shot weights that fishermen used – the swans would eat these along with roots and weed from the bottom of rivers and lakes. Now that fishing weights are made from non-toxic metals, swan poisoning has disappeared and the population is growing again.

Further on, the trees parted overhead and we encountered pine trees on our left, as we approached Loe Bar. This section always reminds me of Greece: with the sea ahead of us, and the pine trees towering over us, all we needed were the cicadas, and some sun. You can almost smell the resin – or at least pretend you can.

Pine trees at Loe Pool

From here we looked down and, instead of some Greek island, saw the end of Loe Pool, the long narrow beach that is Loe Bar, and in the distance, on the far promontory on the right, is a white cross. In December 1807, *HMS Anson* hit bad weather off Mount's Bay, and tried to get to Falmouth harbour but was trapped by wind on the wrong side of the Lizard. The ship anchored but both anchor ropes snapped, so the captain tried to sail the ship onto the centre of Loe Bar. They hit an uncharted reef, 100 metres offshore, and the force of the impact caused the mast to topple onto the beach. Some of the crew escaped along it, but over 100 people drowned. Occasionally gold coins are found here, thought to be from the officers aboard.

One of the men witnessing this was Henry Trengrouse, who was so affected by the helplessness of the onlookers, that he dedicated most of his life and savings to developing the rocket lifesaving apparatus which went on to save many people. This white cross, clearly visible for miles around, acts as a deterrent to those at sea, marks the disaster and also commemorates Henry Trengrouse's wonderful work.

Loe Bar is where the Frenchman and Dona had their last meeting, made a fire from twigs and driftwood, and toasted bread, having no other food. Having rescued him from the gallows, Dona knew that this was the only man she

129

Loe Bar and Pool

would ever love, while he knew he had never loved anyone the way he loved her.

Dona and her French pirate sat, side by side on this strip of sand, by the embers of the fire, and tried to think of a way in which they could be together. He realised that she had killed Rockingham, and had changed as a result: when fighting for her life against Rockingham, Dona forgot to be afraid, and became angry – but it was hearing her son cry that gave her strength. Hearing this, the pirate knew that she could not leave her children. That as man and woman they were too different, with differing needs.

And on the horizon *La Mouette* appeared, with her sails etched against the dawn sky, waiting for her captain to take the boat back to France. (In the book, the Frenchman swims in the pool, but this is not advisable, nor is it recommended to launch a boat from this beach, as happens in the book, as this is a very dangerous area of water.)

Loe Bar was originally the mouth of the River Cober, which led to a harbour in Helston, but by the 13th century the bar had cut Helston off from the sea and formed a pool. Loe Pool, or The Loe, is the largest natural freshwater lake (120 acres) in Cornwall and some six miles if you walk all the way round. Loe Bar is mostly shingle made from chalk flint. It is thought that this bar formed offshore before moving towards the shore, so the bar may not have been there until early mediaeval times.
The bar originally allowed seawater into the lake but mining activity upriver released fine silt that caused it to seal, so it is now freshwater. A disused mine adit is presently used as an overflow from Loe Pool into the sea to prevent parts of Helston flooding. Sometimes the adit has blocked and the Bar has been breached – a practice known locally as 'cutting', to release the build up of water. The last time this happened was in 1984, but the bar has always resealed itself.

However, the story I like better is that Loe Bar was formed with the death of the tyrannical Tregeagle, a steward who abused the poor. His ghost persisted in hanging around so he was given the task of removing sand from one cove to another, sure that the sea would return it. It is said he dropped a sackful of sand at the mouth of the river, and as a result, the Bar and Pool formed.

There are too many fables to list here, but the Helston history website has some wonderful tales, all concerning Loe Bar and Pool, and they are well worth a read.

Loe Bar is renowned for being treacherous: the sea is extremely dangerous and many have drowned, even from paddling. There is a very steep and slippery shingle bank, vicious currents and often very powerful waves, even when calm, with a powerful undertow that can suck people underwater when the shingle disappears beneath their feet. Please don't go near the water or even contemplate swimming here, even when it looks benign. It is rumoured that a freak wave – or the Bar itself – claims a life every seven years, and there is more than a grain of truth in this. It is also the site of several suicides.

When we visited, Loe Bar looked peaceful and sleepy, waves rumbling in the distance, while fishermen stood with their rods, waiting patiently, and several dog walkers strode along the sand. It was only as we walked towards Porthleven, that we noticed the waves crashing onto the shore. Even on a day like ours, with no wind, you could see the force of the water as it clawed its way onto the beach, sucking the sand back like a greedy monster.

Looking out to sea, we could see Poldhu Point, then Predannack Wollas and Lizard Point in the distance. From here you can walk down the slipway onto Loe Bar if you wish, but we stayed on the coastal footpath, walked past Bar Lodge (let out by the National Trust for holidays, if you are interested) towards Porthleven. This part of the path is very close to the cliff, and there is a notice to cyclists and horse riders saying 'Riders Dismount, narrow path', as there is a steep drop down onto an unforgiving sea, so be very careful with young children and dogs.

We could actually smell the salty ozone as we walked along, and were showered with a fine mist of sea spray – and that was when it wasn't even windy, though it was high tide, so be prepared for a soaking in wilder weather.

The inland part of the cliff has subsided in several places, as this is a very popular part of the footpath, so be aware as you walk. Rounding the corner, we saw the coast stretching northwest as far as Mounts Bay and Land's End, with a long line of translucent green waves leaving an elaborate lace frill on the pristine sand. The cottages of Porthleven, nestling amongst the dark green and brown of the cliffside, glowed the same pristine white as the spume sweeping the beaches.

We continued along the path until we came to a bend and saw a waymark sign with a yellow arrow indicating straight on, while blue and red arrows pointed up to the right. We headed up here, inland at 90 degrees, through a metal gate onto a stony steep path edged with a fence on our left and a Cornish hedge on our right. Teasel and the last of the cow parsley gave way to green blackberries in the hedgerows, and some pink campion.

A field of glossy Friesian cattle grazed in a field on our right as the path twisted and turned and we passed other walkers – one lady wearing a smart pair of high heeled sandals and an expensive looking dress, walking head down, avoiding eye contact. "I think she's had an argument with her husband", observed Viv, as we speculated what might have happened – it's a long walk from Porthleven to Penrose in unsuitable shoes.

Coming to another waymark sign, we went right, following the blue and red arrows again. This path doubles back on our route, but higher up, being inland and we were dive bombed by swallows, showing off their aeronautical skills like the Red Arrows. The path turned further inland, with more cow parsley and campion.

We stood and looked down on Loe Bar and the white memorial shining on the cliff top. The tip of Loe Pool was just visible from here, as a grey blue mirror, surrounded by a patchwork of green and yellow fields studded with hay bales. On the horizon we could see Goonhilly Downs with the satellite dishes and windmills next door and walked down a stony path with high hedges on either side.

Two elderly fox gloves emerged from the hedge, having hidden there all summer, but we passed by the blackberries as they looked far too red for me. The path continued to wind round till we came to a metal gate where we crossed a lane and went through another metal gate, following the blue and red waymark signs, and saw a farmhouse ahead.

We continued on, spotting Loe Pool snuggled beneath pine trees on our right, and we approached the farm on our left. Coming to another signpost, you can either walk straight ahead and down into the woods, which will take you back via the Stables cafe, the way we walked in, or go left towards the car park, which is the way we decided to go.

We continued past the granite farmhouse and barns on our left – looking straight out of Jamaica Inn – and the very popular campsite, we crossed the road and headed back down hill to the car park in the trees, while we discussed the ending of *Frenchman's Creek*.

To me this book has everything: strong, empathetic yet flawed characters, a quiet humour, adventure, sword fights, captured ships, and the dangerous possibility of the hero being hanged. While part of me always wishes the ending were happier (I weep every time I read it), it is true to the characters, for the Frenchman is a philosopher, and Dona has become wiser during the magic time they are together. They realise that their time is limited: that they must make the most of it, for it is so precious. And so, with resignation, they talk about how they will age:

"The Lady St Columb will become a gracious matron, and smile upon her servants, and her tenants, and the village folk, and one day she will have grandchildren about her knee, and will tell them the story of a pirate who escaped", Dona says.

Whereas he may stop his piracy and return to his part of Brittany. "It may be that he will go back there again, and cover the bare walls from floor to ceiling with pictures of birds and portraits of his cabin-boy. But as the years go by the portraits of the cabin-boy will become blurred and indistinct."

I still wish that they could at least plan to be together, when her children grow up, and she could leave her dolt of a husband. But du Maurier always knew how to structure her novels, and get the most impact from them – and this one always pierces my heart.

WALK THIRTEEN
MADRON WELL - CORNISH SUPERSTITIONS
From *Vanishing Cornwall*

The Cornish, like most Celts, are a superstitious race, always anxious to protect themselves and their loved ones from evil, and the elements. In Penwith, the term for nightmare is 'hilla-ridden' and a cure for nightmares was to crawl through the Men-an-Tol, an ancient ringed stone, or even better, to bathe in the holy waters of Madron Well. This well has long been revered for its magical healing powers, as well as providing water for the local community.

Apparently John Trelilie had been a cripple all his life and had to walk on his hands, when, in 1650, he dreamed that he must wash himself in Madron Well. He crawled there, and, according to the dream, washed himself three times. He pronounced himself cured, and ever after that, was able to walk on his feet.

Daphne was very taken with the story of John Trelilie, which she relates in her book *Vanishing Cornwall*. This book was written at a time of great turmoil: her husband, Tommy, had just died, she knew she had to leave her beloved Menabilly, and was hoping to move to Kilmarth. Winter was also on its way, and being prone to depression, she dreaded the colder months unless she could write – but this she seemed unable to do, as her imagination "is completely fallow" as she told her publisher.

Then John Sargeant at Doubleday publishers suggested she should write a book about Cornwall, with photographs, which would be part history and part travel. Realising that her beloved son, Kits, could take the photographs, Daphne loved the idea: they could drive around Cornwall researching it, and Daphne could immerse herself in the folklore and history of Cornwall. Being with Kits would also help her while grieving for her husband. And so she started the research for the book, while battling the three devils: grief, depression and winter. At least she had a project to work on, and could look forward to better weather when she and Kits could explore Cornwall.

Daphne had very firm ideas about how the book should be produced, hating the proposed title, 'Romantic Cornwall'. She didn't want a coffee table book, nor a tourist guide, but a book about the history and spirit of Cornwall; the superstitions and legends, and how much the old industries and customs of Cornwall were vanishing.

Both Daphne and Kits spent a magical three weeks driving round Cornwall together, after which he got the pictures developed and contact sheets printed, then sent them to his mother. Finally, in August 1966 she finished the book – she was pleased with it, although she was forced to cut some of the 'anti-tourism' material. She and Kits made a film which came out the following year, just before the book was due, and was shown in London for six weeks, and then on BBC2, to Daphne's delight. The book became a bestseller, with both Kits' photographs and Daphne's prose being praised.

The foreword reads, "To the memory of my husband, because of memories shared and a mutual love of Cornwall; and to our son Christian, who photographed the present, while I rambled on about the past".

What you need to know	
Distance	3 miles
Allow	2 hours
Suggested Map	OS Explorer 102 Land's End
Starting point	Layby; grid reference SW 446323
Terrain	Fairly even
Nearest refreshments	None
Public transport	Atlantic Coaster A17 from Penzance then walk from Madron
Of interest	Madron Well, Celtic Chapel
Facilities	None

Directions

When Daphne and Kits set off to try and find Madron Well, it was difficult to find, so on a still, cold day in November, Mr B, MollieDog and I also set forth, with some trepidation, to look for it.

Coming into Penzance on the A30, we headed up the bypass. At the big roundabout at the top, we took the fourth exit signed to Madron through Heamoor, and drove along the B3312 until we reached Madron. We drove through the village and out the other side and after half a kilometre found a turning on the right saying 'Boswarthen and Wishing Well'. Encouraged, we drove down here and parked in a large layby which was very muddy on the day of our walk.

In the corner of the car park is a small footpath with a granite slate saying 'Celtic Chapel and Wishing Well' by a granite gatepost, and a notice on the right indicating that 'This site is cared for by the Cornish Ancient Sites Protection Network'.

Relieved that we appeared to be on the right track, we headed down this muddy path, me splashing happily in wellies while Mr B leapt like an agile goat dodging puddles - his boots weren't waterproof. "Looks like the wishing well's overflowing", he muttered as the puddles turned into a steady stream, but we had had a lot of rain recently.

It was very peaceful walking along this quiet, almost spooky path, which felt almost like a drowned valley, with a big quarry over on the left. We walked past several huge, fallen yew trees and noted elegant lichen growing on all the branches and trunks.

The path dried out, to Mr B's relief, and was gravelled, when we came to a large area where the stream led into a pond, and cloutie of all kinds hanging from the trees. Cloutie here consisted of a large ornamental glass cross, all different coloured strips of material, shoe laces, bells, ribbons, flannel, a teddy bear, an old sock, bits of lace, a circular item with stars in it, more socks, and a green plastic water bottle. As well as aiding healing, cloutie is supposed to appease the spirits and bring forth cleansing - I felt we should try it for Mr B's sinusitis but he wasn't keen on the idea. He's not a Celt.

There is no proper path to the Well, but it lies about ¼ mile into the boggy area to the left of the cloutie trees, so wellington boots or waders are advisable. If you succeed in getting there, the well is identified by an enclosure of granite slabs, which in wet conditions will be underwater. In fact these stones were erected in the early 1980s, but the well probably originates from pre-Christian times and was here long before the nearby chapel was built.

Many, some infirm or crippled, would come here, often in May to coincide with Beltane, which was the astronomical festival of fertility. Those afflicted

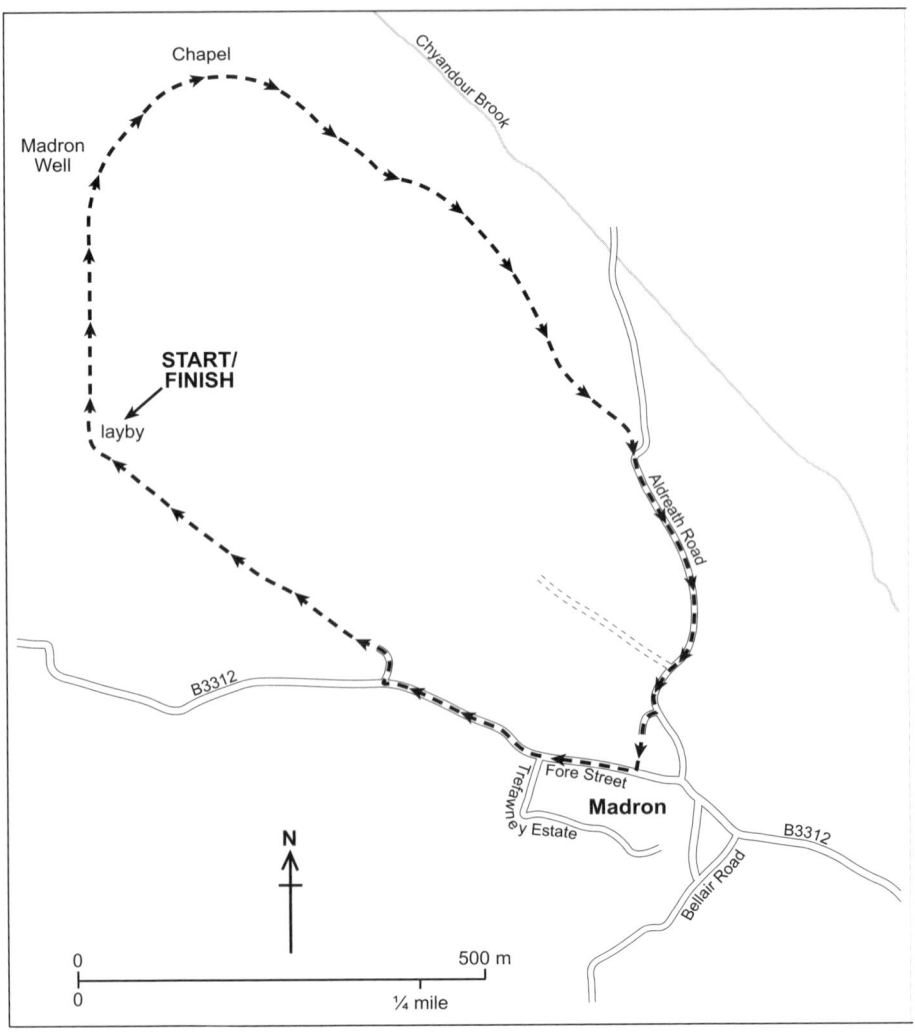

would dip into the water three times, naked, go round the well clockwise three times and then rest on a nearby hill called St Maderne's Bed. They would tear a piece of cloth from the afflicted area, and believed that as the cloth deteriorated, so the ailment would improve. It was thought that the well's unusually high radiation levels were connected to its restorative powers.

Madron Well was also used by the local maidens to find out how soon they would be married. In May, they would visit the Well and make a cross with straw attached by a pin. When placed in the water, the number of bubbles would signify the years they would have to wait. This practice, along with offerings of straw crosses and pins for all manner of wishes, continued well into the 20th century.

From the cloutie trees, we continued along the path to the right where, underneath an old yew tree, we found the remains of the Celtic Chapel. Water ran into the corner of the well, which originally came from the source of the Holy Well, but nowadays contains water from surrounding fields. People had thrown in coins, flowers and shells, I noted – and as I overbalanced, nearly threw myself in. It was a bit cold for my liking, though it might have brought forth cleansing.

Ferns peeped from the ancient stones as we took in the big slab of granite that was the altar, and I wondered how many women had brought children here to be cured. How many men had staggered here, or crawled, like poor John Trelilie? What services did they conduct here, and when, I wondered? What did Daphne make of it when she was here?

Researching later, I found that this chapel had a doorway to the north (which is unusual in Christian

Well in Celtic Chapel

churches as it is sometimes considered the Devil's Door), a large granite altar to the east and a simple stone font in the southwest corner. Although this chapel is dedicated to St Madern, it is believed that it was originally used for pre-Christian pagan worship.

Having left the chapel behind we continued along this path and found a map indicating a circular route between Madron village and Madron chapel. Continuing along the path as indicated, we came to an avenue of firs, with all the branches growing straight up rather than out or along. This stretch of trees stretched for an impressive distance so we wondered who had planted them, why and when. The branches squeaked and groaned above us sounding quite eerie – I wouldn't want to do this walk at dusk, or in the dark. It was almost as if they were trying to tell us tales of people and places gone by and I wished I'd been able to record them.

Boswarthen farmhouse loomed up on the hill on our left, as we headed north, while a buzzard hovered overhead. Two tors loomed up on our left, marked by a Beacon on the map - and a place called Bay of Biscay! Leaving the avenue of trees behind, we continued along the well worn path into a field with a blackthorn hedge on our left, and dessicated bracken. Over a stile we found ourselves in another field and on our left in the distance we could see the West Penwith Moors, with St Michael's Mount beyond. Further still was the Lizard, sticking out in the distance, while over to our far right were Tregonning and Godolphin Hills.

Avenue of squeaky trees

Continuing into the next field, there was a huge bang from what sounded like a metal roof, which frightened MollieDog, though it turned out to be someone shooting – rabbits possibly. Ahead of us loomed a farmhouse and we walked into another field seeing more houses ahead of us. St Michael's Mount was now clearly visible on our left, to the south east, and just before the houses was a gate on the left which we walked through and turned right into a small road with houses on our right – this was the outskirts of the village of Madron.

Further on, two beautiful granite gateposts with a unicorn on the coat of arms denoted the King George V sports field on our right, dated 1910-1930. A big fat pigeon stared at us from a hedge as we walked along, passing the remains of rose hip bushes, and a flock of sparrows tweeting loudly from someone's garden. Looking up a collective noun for a group of sparrows, I found out they can be called a host, a quarrel, a knot, a flutter or a crew. In this instance I rather like 'quarrel' as that's what they sounded like, all arguing cheerfully among themselves.

Madron village seemed peaceful as we walked along Aldreath Road, with rows of well tended cottages. We emerged onto the main road, by the bus stop, where we turned right, back on the road we'd driven in on, walking past sturdy granite miners' cottages. There is a pleasant ancient, cared for feeling to the village, untouched by much of modern trappings. A Methodist church appeared on our left, and the Trelawney housing estate further on.

Coming to the Commonwealth War Graves on the left, and at a row of cottages on our right, we found a very friendly fellow called Clive, refurbishing one of said houses. He provided us with information about where Mr B could get materials for his bathroom, and me with a few contacts in St Ives for where I might sell my books. Though as he admitted, "I don't read, myself. I collect art".

Leaving the village behind us, we came to a public footpath sign on our right and climbed over a large granite stile into a field where we met several other dog walkers. Skirting the right hand side of the field, we climbed over another granite stile noting the granite strewn hillside on our right. It felt rather like a pilgrims' way – for this must have been the route villagers had taken from Madron and further: a grandmother with a painful leg; a sick auntie or cousin, brother or sister, wife or husband, all hoping to be cured at the famous well.

Over another granite stile we came to a muddy path, with a granite trough in the hedge on our left with gorse hedges on both sides, forming an archway of gorse and blackthorn. Further on we came to another granite stile and found ourselves back at the road we drove in on, and the sign to Boswarthen and

Winter sky at Madron

Wishing Well. From here we reached the layby where we'd parked the car, and reflected what a gentle, peaceful walk this is, with no steep hills but plenty of Celtic history.

The Well, like many around Cornwall, is a place of mystery with the suggestion of magic. This is where women brought their children to cure them of shingles and other childhood illnesses, and to guard them against the evil eye. Stand in amongst the cloutie hanging from the branches, and feel the presence of all those wishes. Visit the chapel and wonder at the services of the past, of those who visited it, and what magic and healing took place. There is a definite sense of a world of which we have no tangible knowledge. No wonder Daphne was so taken with it.

WALK FOURTEEN
THE LEGEND OF PENROSE
A story of murder and betrayal from *Vanishing Cornwall*

"What remains of the old mansion of Penrose, in Sennen, stands on a low and lonely site at the head of a narrow valley through which a mill-brook winds, with many abrupt turns, for about three miles, thence to Penberth Cove." This excerpt, from Taylor's Hearthside Stories, caught Du Maurier's interest – or rather, the story associated with it.

Some 300 years ago, the Penrose family lived in this mansion house in the parish of Sennen. The head of the family was Ralph Penrose, a recently widowed smuggler whose wife had died of a fever. Ever since, Ralph hated being on land and spent more and more time at sea, taking his seven year old son with him and leaving his brother, John, to look after the estate.

One winter's night, when Ralph's ship was returning home, a gale blew up off Land's End, the ship struck the Cowloe rocks and Ralph and all his crew (and son) ended up in the water. They sent flares up so John Penrose came down to Sennen Cove and heard the shouts from the drowning men, but, it was rumoured, did nothing to save them. So everyone on board died except Ralph's young son, the heir to the estate.

John appointed himself guardian to his nephew and behaved as if the estate were his. But after that terrible night, John took to drink and wild ways, leaving the fisherfolk of Sennen terrified for their wives and daughters. Having lost his brother, he became terrified of the sea, and had a sturdy vessel built with a captain and crew who developed a truly evil reputation for piracy. When the ship was berthed, John would invite the crew and captain to drink long and hard at Penrose.

One snowy winter night, word came that wolves had been spotted on the commons above Penrose, and everyone, including the young boy, rushed off to see them, leaving John and the captain drinking. Returning, the servants could find no sign of the young heir and, despite endless searching of the cliffs and Sennen Cove, his body was not found. Everyone presumed that he'd fallen into the sea and drowned.

The household entered mourning for the young lad, except for John Penrose who gambled heavily, drank to greater excess, and put the fear of God into everyone with his even wilder behaviour. But strangely, he would have nothing more to do with the captain, who gave in his notice and disappeared from the area.

A year later, on the anniversary of the lad's death, a stranger came knocking at the door of Penrose. He was fed and watered, and the steward told him how strange and evil things had happened over the past year, ever since the young heir had died. The stranger was given a bed in the old wing of the house, and from there, watched the New Year's revelries outside. Suddenly, there was a piercing scream as a great wall of fog came rolling in, and then came the sound of the sea, which was strange as the sea was a mile or more away.

All the revellers fled indoors as the storm approached. Waves crashed onto the rocks, timbers splintered and breakers crashed in on the courtyard, carrying a longboat of men, shouting, "save us!". As the boat overturned, the crew all landed in the water, drowning, but one man looked up at the window where the stranger stood, and shouted, "William Penrose, arise and avenge the murder of your cousin's son!"

Then everything went quiet. The voices, the sea and the fog disappeared, as did the drowning men, and the courtyard was silent and deserted as before.

The stranger was, indeed, cousin William Penrose, believed to have drowned with Ralph in the shipwreck, when in fact he had been washed ashore but lost his memory and wandered around the countryside, until something made him head for home. While William tossed and turned in bed, hearing the instructions to avenge the death of his cousin's son, he heard a young voice whisper in his ear, "My uncle bade the captain murder me. I lie beneath the dead tree in the orchard. Dig and you shall find me. Dig, and place my bones in Sennen churchyard. Dig, and give me peace at last."

William finally tracked the captain down in Plymouth: he was tormented with remorse and lay dying but confessed to having killed the boy, not just for the money that John Penrose paid him, but because he had loved the boy's mother, and when she married Ralph, the devil had entered his heart. The captain then died (conveniently), and William returned to Penrose and went to the orchard where he and the steward found the dead tree and dug until they uncovered the boy's remains. Secretly, they carried him to Sennen churchyard in the dark and buried him properly.

When William returned to Penrose he found the door of the malthouse below the manor wide open and the body of John Penrose swinging from a beam – he'd hanged himself in sight of the dead tree in the orchard.

Sadly, William found the place so infested with ghosts that he couldn't stay there, so he relinquished his rights to the house and went off to the Holy Land. After that, most of the original house was pulled down and today it is a farm, and a listed building.

In her book *Vanishing Cornwall*, Du Maurier describes her visit to Penrose, with her son, Kits.

He was concerned that reality might not live up to the story that his mother had read; that her fertile imagination had once more leapt ahead, and that she would be bitterly disappointed when they actually got there – and maybe would found no sign of the old house.

As Kits drove, his mother told him the story, embellishing it as only she could; bringing the story to life. (Do read this chapter – she tells it so convincingly.) They finally found the farmhouse, which looked solid and respectable. The orchard was no more, but a desolate, marshy meadow. With a singular tree standing in the middle.

What you need to know	
Distance	4½ miles
Allow	3 hours approximately
Suggested Map	OS Explorer 102 Land's End
Starting point	Treen Campsite; grid reference SW 395230
Terrain	Reasonably even, quite a few stiles, several fields of cattle

Nearest refreshments	Treen Cafe – April to October, 10am-4pm also The Logan Rock Inn
Public transport	www.cornwallpublictransport.info/bus_maps.asp
Of interest	Dog friendly year round
Facilities	Toilets near campsite

Directions

One overcast Saturday, Heather, MollieDog and I headed to Penzance and from there took the A30 towards Land's End. At Catchall we turned left, onto the B3283, towards St Buryan and continued to the B3315. We turned right onto St Buryan Hill and then turn left at Treen Hill, going past the Logan Rock Inn. We continued round to the left where we found the Treen campsite car park: parking was £2 all day at time of walking. There are also toilets here and the Treen cafe selling ice creams, crab sandwiches; and dogs get a free bonio.

Walking out of the car park, we passed a red phone box which now houses a defibrillator, ignored the public footpath sign on the left and walked down past the Logan Rock Inn, then Treen Farm with lots of chickens clucking in the distance, back to the main road. Here we turned right, down the hill, past a stall selling bunches of brilliant orange calendula and took the first public footpath sign on the left at the bottom of the hill.

This led NW along a rough track with grass growing down the middle, past several houses, an allotment, and dense woodlands on our left. Bursts of orange montbretia brightened the hedges as we continued along this path, crossing a stream as we passed a collection of outhouses and a small fibre glass boat marooned on the grass. Heading slightly uphill, we came to a bracken covered hillside with mossy grass and looked down to see the flowers that were sold in the stall – bright orange and yellow marigolds, red, pinks and purples of sweet peas cheering the garden. Beyond that was the wooded Penberth valley – unusual for Cornwall to see such dense trees, particularly near the coast.

Along here was a well hidden lower path on the left but we went straight ahead and continued walking with a hedge on our left, noticing the first green sloes, campion and baby ferns, while underfoot was trefoil (bacon and egg) and clover, with overgrown fields on our right. The woody smell of wet bracken accompanied us as we passed through a gate and a well defined path leading through a field of tall maize, like a jungle. In the distance was the mewing sound of a buzzard, which we then saw wheeling above us, while a tractor rumbled in the next field.

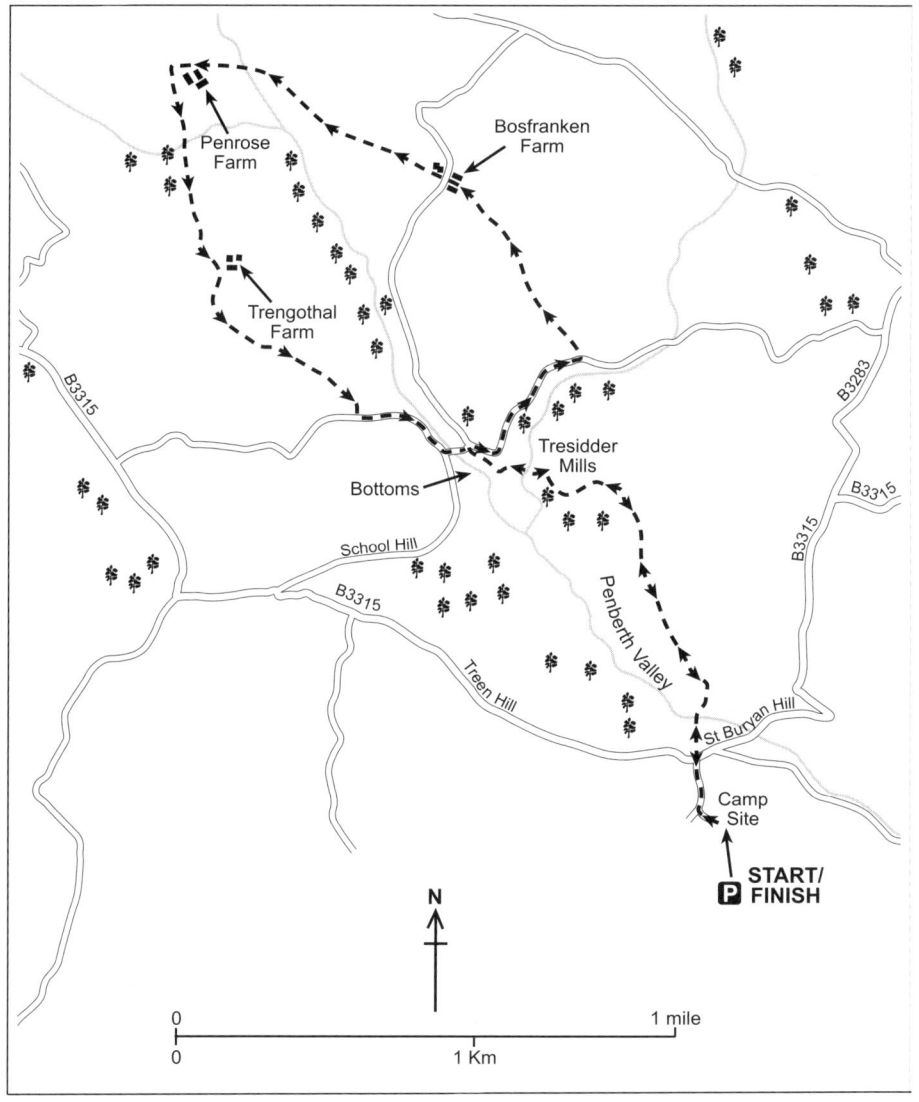

Continuing, we found ourselves in another field of maize, while the sky hung above us heavy and swollen with unshed rain. This path led over a fallen metal five barred gate, into a muddy farm lane with massive granite boulders forming a new wall to the farm and outbuildings on our left. There were no house signs or waymark signs at the time of walking, but at a small junction just past the farm we turned sharp left down an old driveway past The Old Cattle Shed and Tresidder Farmhouse and other renovated barns while a swallow dive bombed over our heads.

We inhaled the sweet, pungent scent of camomile as we walked along, past a huge, lilac coloured hydrangea. Walking downhill into a wooded area with pine needles underfoot and sycamore trees on our right, Heather did a sterling job map reading, while I juggled tape recorder, lead and camera. Down below on our left we could hear a stream rushing by as we walked past a pearly pink and blue hydrangea, as the track then led uphill, carved out of the hillside.

A huge buzzard flew out of the woods, over our heads, as we came to a wooden house on stilts and we found ourselves at Crean Bottoms, the junction of a small road where we turned right, NW, ignoring the left turn, and followed the road uphill towards Crean. Magpies cackled overhead as we climbed the steep hill, noting stray spuds along the side of the road.

Soon we came to a public footpath sign, almost hidden by the hedge, on our left, past Cave Cottage and a stack of logs, up the hill, while pigeons cooed overhead. Here we met a very friendly lady wielding a wicker basket full of books on design and textiles. When we told her about this book, she was very interested, and said she believed that Penrose and Bosfranken farmhouses and many other dwellings round here are owned and leased out by the Lord Falmouth's Tregothnan Estate – one of the biggest landowners in the country.

Heading towards Bosfranken Farm, we climbed over an overgrown granite stile and walked along with the field boundary on our left, and a field on our right. As it had just rained, there was a lovely smell of wet earth and wet grass as we continued over another stile, and on to another stile, with a wind turbine turning lazily ahead.

At the corner of the next field we clambered over yet another stile by a tree, and made our way across the next field with Bosfranken Farm ahead of us. Arriving here, we asked directions from the farmer's wife who said we should climb over the stile in the corner of their yard and follow the stiles towards

Penrose. There are no waymark signs here, but we walked diagonally across the next field with some satellite dishes and wind turbines ahead, and Sennen church in the west up to our left.

At the end of this field we turned left, downhill, over a stile in the right hand side of the field, then into the next field where we saw a wooden stile in the left hand hedge, a few yards further on. Here we stopped for our sandwiches and watched a couple of wagtails dancing in the field. Emerging into the next field, we walked diagonally to the right and saw a cantilevered stile partly hidden by gorse and nettles leading into yet another field.

From here we could see Penrose ahead of us and walked straight across the field towards an opening at the far end. The field below Penrose was very boggy and full of reeds so be careful where you walk. Heading towards the gateway, we climbed over a stile into a field below Penrose which led to a gateway and another stile that led us to the track outside Penrose.

The house, which dates back to 1300, is long and solid, with granite walls, well cared for with white painted iron gates leading to the front door. There is no obvious road to the farm which sits in splendid isolation, surrounded by barns – no sign of any ghosts, cobbled courtyards or any hint of

Penrose House

wickedness about the place. It was apparently once the greatest manor in Penwith, and according to the BBC Domesday site, "a house of piracy and smuggling".

According to the BBC Domesday Reloaded site, a Mrs Hoskins, who lived here in 1986, claimed that Penrose was frequented by ghosts. She said, "I felt a presence in the room, of a tall man, bending over a cot. I called out, "what do you want?". There was no reply, but then I sensed he was standing over my bed. Although I could not lift my hand to put on the light, I did not feel afraid. But what was odd was that although the presence was that of a man, I seem to remember the rustling of robes." Daphne would have loved talking to this lady, but she lived there after Daphne had visited, and written the book.

As I was taking pictures of the house, a young farmer appeared – this was Antony Hosking, whose family has lived here for 120 years – he was born and brought up here. Very kindly he said he would point us in the right direction for our return journey, so we followed the waymark sign on the right, round the back of the house, and further on another waymark sign pointing left, almost due south.

As Heather was chatting to Antony, I did look down towards the stream, which is apparently where the orchard was. However, there was no sign of any lone oak or elm in the middle of the field that Daphne and her son saw, under which the young Penrose son was buried. Only a group of cattle who eyed us – or Moll – with interest, before continuing to munch.

We walked downhill, by the left hand side of the field with a stone hedge, following a path beaten through the grass, and found a wooden gate over a stile in the corner. This led into another field and we headed down towards a small wooded area where we found a granite footbridge into the woods. Antony had warned us that it might be overgrown here – it was rather like a jungle but manageable, though a stick would have been useful to beat back the brambles. Antony had also told us about some slippery boardwalks so we walked over these gingerly until we came to a field where we headed diagonally along a defined path by the field boundary towards a barn at the top of the hill.

Climbing over a stile to the right of the barn, we turned left, through Trengothal Farm and outbuildings and followed the road round. We were high up, here, looking over to the isolated tower of St Buryan church east in the

Gingerbread House

distance, while we looked back towards Penrose which had disappeared from view, cleverly tucked away so that no one would know where it was.

Walking along, bearing to the left, we came to a field of the most beautiful Jersey cows – "with eyeliner and mascara" as Heather pointed out. They were also very keen on having their picture taken and clustered by the fence while I obliged. Further on, the hedges loomed high on either side of us full of holly, bracken, ash and sycamore trees. Soon we came to a junction where we turned left by a thatched cottage with a fox on top – this is the thatcher's own distinctive mark. Walking round, we noticed a pheasant on the other side – this is a real gingerbread house, with the prettiest fairytale garden to match.

Continuing, we came to an overgrown orchard laden with apple trees and acers about to turn. We passed another granite house with very tall chimneys and an almost sub tropical huge garden, with the Penberth stream running through it. Soon we came to the Crean Bottoms junction we'd arrived at earlier, and turned left, to find the house on stilts. From here we walked back along the route we'd taken earlier, through the maize fields and finally back to the Treen cafe where we had a very welcome coffee and hot chocolate – though take note that they only open April to October.

While we relaxed with our drinks and a piece of very good lemon cake, we mulled over the hidden secrecy of yet another wonderful Cornish farmhouse, and the extraordinary tale that surrounded it. Who uprooted the lone tree, I wondered, where the little boy was initially buried? Are there still ghosts at Penrose house? Was the orchard where the marshy meadow is now?

I'd like to go back and find the answers to these questions – any excuse to revisit this still undiscovered part of Cornwall. I feel sure that Daphne du Maurier would be pleased to know Penrose is still standing, so well cared for and still a working farm, with the same family there as when she visited. Long may it continue.

Also from Sigma Leisure:

Walks in the Footsteps of Winston Graham's Poldark
Sue Kittow

Walks in the Footsteps of Winston Graham's Poldark features 12 walks each associated with a different Poldark location from the books, a character, or where an event was filmed for the TV series. Winston Graham was so good at evoking the real landscape of Cornwall, the Cornish people and the unpredictability of the Cornish weather. Feature in page turning plots and empathetic characters, and you have a winner, which the Poldark books have proved to be.

Enjoy these walks and learning more about the Poldark places, characters, and history. Each walk includes details of maps, refreshments, history, points of interest and clear directions and sketch map. What makes these walks different is their personal style, the delightful details and excellent photographs, which combine to make this a unique book to keep and pore over.

£8.99

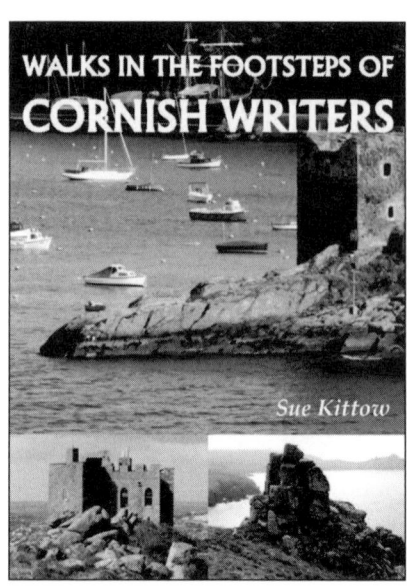

Walks in the Footsteps of Cornish Writers
Sue Kittow

Walks in the Footsteps of Cornish Writers features 20 walks each associated with different writers connected to Cornwall. It has been fascinating talking to the contemporary authors about their favourite walks. Similarly, it has been interesting to find out more about the places that were so special to those well known writers who are no longer with us - and why they were so special.

Some writers, like John Betjeman, have made their favourite places famous through verse or novels. Others, like Philip Marsden, use regular walks as a valuable part of their writing day, and it has been a privilege to share their thoughts. From Derek Tangye's books based in Lamorna to the Reverend Stephen Hawker at Morwenstow, here are a variety of walks that inspired the authors, and I hope will inspire readers too.

Each walk has an introduction, a factbox with all essential information, and details of maps, refreshments, history, points of interest and clear directions.
£8.99

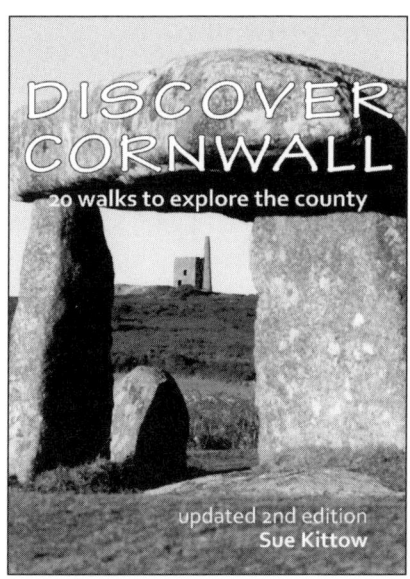

Discover Cornwall
20 walks to explore the county
Sue Kittow

Cornwall's fine golden sands have provided the backdrop for many childhood holidays, but it is also a coastal footpath, there are numerous less known routes that are great fun to investigate.

There are a good range of gentle to moderate walks between 4 and 6 miles in length. Discover Cornwall lists 20 walks providing a healthy and entertaining way to keep fit, learn about Cornwall, and enjoy the beaches, moorland and hisotry of this magical county.

The walks have clear directions, delightful details and excellent photographs, maing this a unique book to keep and pore over for readers as well as walkers.
£8.99

Rainy Days in Cornwall
Jean Patefield

Cornwall has a long and beautiful coastline, with wonderful beaches many of which are excellent for surfing. There are also picturesque valleys and woodland. Overall it merits its place as the premier summer resort in Britain.Unfortunately, being in the west of England, even in high summer wind and rain can lash the beaches, the temperature can plummet and the coast can be shrouded in mist and drizzle. What should one do when your week's summer holiday is turning into a disaster? Carry on regardless, huddled behind a windbreak trying to keep warm or patronise the numerous attractions and spend a fortune? Rainy Days in Cornwall offers a solution to this problem with twenty suggestions of free and interesting things to do in Cornwall in less than perfect weather.
£8.99

Cornwall Walking on the level
Norman & June Buckley

This book selects and illustrates 28 routes, mainly circular, which explore some of the finest parts of the county, without serious ascent. In addition to the route directions, the distance, ascent, car parking, refreshment and map, with a succinct assessment, are provided for each walk.
£8.99

South West England Nature Walks
from train stations
Graeme Down

Get away from it all and find nature using the train! Although the countryside is easily accessible by car, it's far more relaxing to combine the beauty of the countryside with the less stressful mode of train travel. 24 circular walks, two walks for each month of the year, timed to give maximum chance of spotting the wildlife on offer. Each route is clearly described and accompanied by a map. Along the way, hints are given to help the reader identify some of the wildlife they may be able to find.
£8.99

Dorset Accessible Walks
25 accessible walks in the beautiful county of Dorset
Marie Houlden

For each walk there is a brief description and then more detailed information about distance, gradient and terrain, allowing the reader to make an informed decision about the suitability of their equipment and their own particular needs. All of the walks are stile and obstacle free, with consideration given to those in wheelchairs, including information on disabled parking spots and accessible facilities. With walks that start from only a mile and that cover a mixture of terrain and environments, there really is something for everyone. There are even a couple of more strenuous walks for those with an all-terrain pushchair and a passion for a physical challenge!
£8.99

Walking in and around Hampshire's Meon Valley
Louis Murray

The river Meon is one of Hampshire's quintessential chalk streams. It rises from natural springs in the South Downs to the south of the village of East Meon. This book contains the details of 20 walks in the Meon river valley area in southern Hampshire. The walks are suitable for novices, casual walkers, family groups, and experienced ramblers.
£8.99

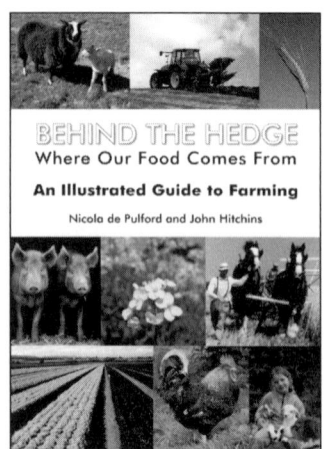

Behind the Hedge
Where Our Food Comes From
An Illustrated Guide to Farming
Nicola de Paulford & John Hitchins

For everyone who wants to know more about the food we eat, the land it is grown and reared on, and those who farm it. This fully illustrated easy-to-follow colour guide will help you identify in their natural environment our crops, fruit and farm animals, agricultural buildings and machinery, the farming landscape and the wildlife it supports. Never again will you mistake a field of wheat for one of barley, or an Aberdeen Angus cow for a Hereford. .
£12.99

All of our books are all available on-line at **www.sigmapress.co.uk** or through booksellers.

**Sigma Leisure, Stobart House, Pontyclerc, Penybanc Road, Ammanford, Carmarthenshire SA18 3HP
Tel: 01269 593100 Fax: 01269 596116
info@sigmapress.co.uk www.sigmapress.co.uk**